LIFEWAY IN-DEPTH BIBLE STUDY

James

HOW TO LIVE BY FAITH IN A SECULAR WORLD

The Letter of James

LifeWay Press®
Nashville, Tennessee

ISBN 1-4158-5277-4
Item 005035518

This book is a resource in the Bible Studies category of the Christian Growth Study Plan.
Course CG-1198

Dewey Decimal Classification: 227.91
Subject Headings: BIBLE. N.T. JAMES—STUDY AND TEACHING

To order additional copies of this resource:
WRITE LifeWay Church Resources Customer Service;
One LifeWay Plaza; Nashville, TN 37234-0113; FAX order to (615) 251-5933;
PHONE (800) 458-2772; ORDER ONLINE at *www.lifeway.com;*
or VISIT the LifeWay Christian Store serving you.

Printed in the United States of America

Leadership and Adult Publishing
LifeWay Church Resources
One LifeWay Plaza
Nashville, TN 37234-0175

Contents

Leader Guide

This guide is designed to help you as you study and lead LifeWay In-depth Bible Study: *James*. This study is comprised of 4 units divided into 8 lessons. These lessons reflect the content and organization of the Book of James.

The ultimate purpose of this study is to lead you and the other learners in your Bible study group to thoroughly know the Book of James, including its background information and author through verse by verse explanations.

However, knowledge of the Bible must result in godly attitudes and actions. Allow God to do His work in the transformation of your heart as you read His Word. Application of these truths to life should be a significant part of your group sessions.

Just as James wanted his readers to be a spiritual people, God wants to encourage your group to grow in spiritual maturity. May God bless you as you study and teach this material.

How to Use This Resource

This material is not organized around a one-hour Bible study format. The lessons may cover more or fewer verses than can be taught within any one particular group session.

In other words, we recommend that you proceed through this material at the pace that seems right for your group. If your session time is over before you complete an entire lesson, simply mark your stopping place and begin your next session at that point.

The commentary is found only in this leader book. All the learners need to bring are their Bibles. Teaching suggestions are located in the colored boxes following each point in the outline. These boxes include Content Points, Discussion Questions, and Application Ideas to guide lecture and discussion.

In addition, outline and related discussion questions are on the CD-ROM PowerPoint™ presentation accompanying this book. Use the Discussion Questions to jumpstart your thinking on ways to promote interaction with your Bible study group.

As you read the Application Ideas, reflect on your own life experiences to help you personalize the Scripture and apply it to your life and to the lives of the learners.

Occasionally you will find interactive learning activities meant just for you. Stop and complete them before continuing with your reading to help maximize your understanding and application of the verses.

These activities are in addition to those found in the colored boxes. They represent insights that are more personal in nature. You may choose to use some of these with your group. Related verses from other books of the Bible are placed in the margins of each lesson too.

Getting the Most Out of Your Study

As you prepare, pause and reflect on each paragraph. In the margin jot down thoughts and feelings you have as you are led by the Holy Spirit. The Content Points will also be helpful in organizing the lessons around concepts and themes.

Do not limit your ideas to those found in the commentary. Consider the personalities and needs of those in the group. Some group members will talk or read portions of the Bible aloud. Others may wish to listen in silence.

Personal questions should always be answered only on a volunteer basis. The degree to which you are comfortable sharing your life experiences will be reflected by the group.

Additional study materials for each lesson are labeled **Going Deeper.** These sections provide helpful information for understanding difficult concepts, words, or verses; they are referenced only in this commentary. The **Going Deeper** sections are not a part of the PowerPoint™ outline.

Importance of Prayer and Bible Reading

Remember how important it is to walk with God in prayer, taking in daily guidance from the Holy Spirit as we seek to become Christlike in all we say and do. Encourage prayer as a dynamic part of each session.

Don't limit yourself to prayer before and/or after the session. Pray at points in the outline where a recognized need is found. Rejoice in prayer as you read James's words of encouragement.

Some groups will want to have designated prayer partners who will pray for each other every week. Others will assign prayer partners for a month or so before assigning new partners. This approach encourages building friendships among the members. Pair women with women and men with men.

The printed Scripture in the Leader Guide is provided in the Holman Christian Standard Bible® translation. If group members do not have this particular translation, encourage them to refer to their own Bibles when a new passage is introduced. Perhaps a variety of translations will help in clarifying each verse, so instruct your group to use their own Bibles as you teach.

Encourage daily Bible reading. Suggest that members follow the plan to read the Bible in a year. Or ask them to reread the Book of James from 1:1 to the point where you stopped last. As you near the end, suggest that they read the entire Book of James in one sitting.

Christian Growth Study Plan

Persons who complete the course of study for *James* are eligible for Christian Growth Study Plan credit from LifeWay Christian Resources.

During the last session provide photocopies of the Christian Growth Study Plan form on page 160. After the members have filled out the forms, mail them to the address found on the form.

CD-ROM

The CD-ROM accompanying this leader guide is for class use. You may download and print copies of the PowerPoint™ portions you will be covering in the next session. These pages may then serve as a participant's guide on which to make notes and answer the discussion questions.

If you are using the PowerPoint™ as a teaching outline in class, have the necessary equipment to project it on a screen or facing wall. Encourage participants to take notes.

The articles from *Biblical Illustrator* can be duplicated for participants, or they may serve as background information for you as you plan each week's lesson.

For advertising purposes you can print a page from the CD-ROM and enlarge it for a poster. The map contained in the file would also make a good poster for use throughout the study.

The contents of the CD-ROM are as follows:

PowerPoint™
James: How to Live by Faith in a Secular World

Map:
Churches Who May Have Received the Book of James

Articles from *Biblical Illustrator*
The Canonization in the Book of James
James's Audience
Patience in James
The First Century Church and Poverty
Judgment in James

For Further Study

We hope that your study of *James* will lead the group to choose another of the LifeWay In-depth Bible Study series. To order *LifeWay In-depth Bible Study: Ephesians, God's Special People* refer to the Copyright page (p. 2) for information.

These studies are compiled from material owned by LifeWay Press and do not represent the work of a single author.

James Outline

INTRODUCTION:

I. UNIT ONE: GROW UP! (James. 1:1-27)

Lesson One: Learn from Tests and Trials (vv. 1-18)
Lesson Two: Examine Your Life by God's Word (vv. 19-27)

II. UNIT TWO: BEHAVE YOURSELF! (James. 2:1-26)

Lesson Three: Treat All People Right (vv. 1-13)
Lesson Four: Demonstrate Your Faith (vv. 14-26)

III. UNIT THREE: SERVE OTHERS! (James. 3:1-4:17)

Lesson Five: Seek Power Over Yourself, Not Over Others (3: 1-18)
Lesson Six: Seek What Is Best for Others, Not for Yourself (4:1-17)

IV. UNIT FOUR: TRUST GOD! (James. 5:1-20)

Lesson Seven: Endure Patiently (vv. 1-12)
Lesson Eight: Pray Confidently (vv. 13-20)

Introduction to James

The Letter of James was written to confront problems the apostle saw among the 12 tribes scattered throughout the Mediterranean world and beyond. James had a practical purpose in writing: to lead Christians to reject secular values and to live instead by genuine Christian values. Worldliness hindered the Lord's work then and still does so today. This letter has great relevance for us as we struggle with the temptations of a secular culture.

A. Human Author—The author identifies himself as "James, a slave of God and of the Lord Jesus Christ" (Jas. 1:1). Four people named James appear in the New Testament, including James, the father of Judas and James the son of Alphaeus (Matt. 10:3,31; Luke 6:15-16; Mark 3:18). Neither would have been able to describe himself simply as "James, a slave of God and of the Lord Jesus Christ" (Jas. 1:1). Another candidate, James the son of Zebedee and brother of John (the "Sons of thunder" in Mark 3:18), was a prominent leader, but he was martyred around A.D. 41 (Acts 12:2)—almost certainly before the letter was written to "the Dispersion" of believers (Jas. 1:1).

The most probable author is James the half brother of Jesus (Mark 6:3), although he was not a believer until after the resurrection (John 7:5). The letter's vocabulary indicates Jesus' words influenced the author (compare Jas. 4:11 with Matt. 7:1-2). Also, the wording is similar to James's speech at the Jerusalem Conference (Acts 15:13-21).

The James described in early Christian writings was deeply spiritual and concerned about keeping the Jewish law, maintaining integrity and morality, and denouncing a faith that did not produce good works. All of these issues appear in the letter. James's position as leader of the Jerusalem church gave him a strong platform from which to write such a bold letter to believers.

B. First Readers—James addressed the letter "To the 12 tribes in the Dispersion" (Jas. 1:2). This phrase usually described Israel, God's chosen people. At least three times in their history large numbers of Jews had been forcibly removed from their homeland. Some also left for commercial reasons. Thus Jews lived and flourished all over the Mediterranean world and beyond.

Had James written to all scattered Jews about Christianity, surely he would have presented arguments to prove Jesus was the Messiah. Instead he wrote about how Christians are to live, obviously indicating the first readers were believers. Many Jews, like James, had received Christ and still participated in their synagogues and honored Jewish law and tradition.

"The 12 tribes in the Dispersion," however, could have been his way of addressing believers of all nationalities as true Israel. Jews who had rejected Jesus as the Messiah no longer could lay claim to the title (see Rom. 9:6-8; Gal. 3:6-9). Likely James was referring to people everywhere who had received Jesus as the Christ.

C. Date—Many Bible scholars believe James's letter is the earliest New Testament writing. The latest possible date for the letter is around A.D. 62, the traditional date for James's martyrdom. But how long before that was this letter written? The fact that the letter contains no reference to the vital problem dealt with at the Jerusalem Conference (Acts 15) suggests it probably was written before that conference took place in A.D. 50, likely in A.D. 49-50.]

D. Place in the Canon—Under the leadership of the Holy Spirit, the books of the canon were recognized as inspired by virtue of their value to the churches. The Letter of James is one of the seven New Testament writings called "General Epistles" because they were not addressed to a particular congregation or person. These letters were among the last accepted into the canon.

E. Contents—This letter gives general instructions on a number of ethical subjects. Some Bible scholars see a rather closely reasoned relationship between the subjects; others see the book more as a collection of lessons on different topics. The organization of this particular in-depth study reflects the first view, the relationship between subjects.

JAMES 1:1-18 (HCSB)

*[1]James, a slave of God and of the Lord Jesus Christ: To the 12
tribes in the Dispersion. Greetings. [2]Consider it a great joy, my
brothers, whenever you experience various trials, [3]knowing
that the testing of your faith produces endurance. [4]But endurance must do its complete work, so that you may be mature and
complete, lacking nothing.*

*[5]Now if any of you lacks wisdom, he should ask God, who
gives to all generously and without criticizing, and it will be given
to him. [6]But let him ask in faith without doubting. For the doubter
is like the surging sea, driven and tossed by the wind. [7]That person
should not expect to receive anything from the Lord.*

*[8]An indecisive man is unstable in all his ways. [9]The brother
of humble circumstances should boast in his exaltation; [10]but
the one who is rich |should boast| in his humiliation, because he
will pass away like a flower of the field. [11]For the sun rises with its
scorching heat and dries up the grass; its flower falls off, and its
beautiful appearance is destroyed. In the same way, the rich man
will wither away while pursuing his activities.*

*[12]Blessed is a man who endures trials, because when he passes
the test he will receive the crown of life that He has promised to
those who love Him. [13]No one undergoing a trial should say, "I am
being tempted by God." For God is not tempted by evil, and He
Himself doesn't tempt anyone.*

*[14]But each person is tempted when he is drawn away and
enticed by his own evil desires.*

*[15]Then after desire has conceived, it gives birth to sin, and
when sin is fully grown, it gives birth to death. [16]Don't be deceived,
my dearly loved brothers. [17]Every generous act and every perfect
gift is from above, coming down from the Father of lights; with
Him there is no variation or shadow cast by turning.*

*[18]By His own choice, He gave us a new birth by the message of
truth so that we would be the firstfruits of His creatures.*

Unit one: Grow Up!

Lesson One

LEARN FROM TESTS AND TRIALS (JAMES 1:1-18)

I. Introduction (1:1)

II. Trials Provide Opportunities (1:2-4)

III. Trials Require Wisdom (1:5-8)

IV. Trials Can Be Financial (1:9-12)

A. The Trial of Poverty (v. 9)

B. The Trial of Wealth (vv. 10-11)

C. The Payoff of Enduring Trials (v. 12)

V. Temptations Can Be Overcome (1:13-18)

LEARNING GOALS

As a result of studying this lesson, learners will:

- *Identify the author and first readers of James*
- *Describe the appropriate Christian response to trials*
- *Appreciate their need for wisdom and learn how to get it*
- *Understand the trials brought by both poverty and wealth*
- *Trust God's goodness in times of temptation*

Notes

How do secular worldviews and values affect your life? Assign a number to each area with 1 being not at all to 5 being completely.

- sexually/morally? ___
- integrity/honesty?___
- possessions/materialism?___
- status/social circles/prejudice?___

We live in a secular world, and many of us have accepted more of the world's secular values than we like to admit. Take Audrey for example. She slammed the door after getting into her car. Once more several coworkers had ridiculed her, laughing at her discomfort. Audrey angrily asked herself aloud, "Why are they so rude? Why don't they like me? Why does God let them do such things? Is He behind it?"

An objective outsider could have explained that her pride, ambition, and selfish attitudes resulted in some of her coworkers' cutting remarks. Audrey was blind to the conflict between her secular values and her professed faith in Christ.

In his day James saw a host of Audreys. He saw believers who placed a premium on success, wealth, power, and the satisfaction of physical desires. Too few of them practiced spiritual disciplines, protected other people's rights, met others' needs, or followed biblical guidelines for daily living. Under the Holy Spirit's inspiration, James strongly admonished Christians to live by Christian values.

We are plagued by the same weaknesses, temptations, tendencies, and omissions that James addressed in the first-century. A pastor today could read the Letter of James aloud as his sermon in approximately 15 minutes and hardly speak a word that did not apply directly to virtually every person in the congregation.

James's message has been and will continue to be an intensely relevant challenge to all who want to be effective Christians and purposeful church members. Let us allow God to speak to us through this inspired letter. We will receive the help this book offers when we are tempted to live by the secular values of our world yet effectively resist them.

The first section, James 1:1-18, tells us how we can learn from tests and trials.

1 James, a slave of God and of the Lord Jesus Christ: To the 12 tribes in the Dispersion. Greetings.

I. *Introduction* (1:1)

James (the Greek form of the popular Hebrew name *Jacob*) followed the usual pattern for writing letters in the first century. He identified himself and his readers, and then he expressed "greetings," a term found in thousands of first-century Greek letters.

Most conservative Bible scholars believe the writer was James the half brother of Jesus. Although James was not one of the Twelve, he served as the leader of the Jerusalem church. In this letter he did not identify himself by his physical relationship to Jesus, though he properly could have done so. Instead, he humbly described himself as "a slave of God and of the Lord Jesus Christ."

The earliest readers of James understood that "Christ" meant "Messiah." James acknowledged that he belonged to God and to Jesus Christ. "Slave" expressed his humility and commitment to God in Christ.

James addressed his readers as the 12 tribes in the Dispersion. The term "Dispersion" signified Jews who were outside the holy land and scattered over the Gentile world. The 12 tribes ordinarily referred to the whole nation of Israel. James, however, probably used the term as a symbolic description of the new spiritual Israel, the church, thus including believing Gentiles as well as Jews throughout the Roman Empire. That description applies to believers today.

Content Points

1. James could lay claim to authority and respect in the Jerusalem church because he was its leader: Also, he was the half brother of Jesus.
2. Despite his grounds for boasting, James called himself "a slave" of the Lord Jesus Christ.
3. His audience included believing Jews and Gentiles.

Discussion Questions

1. What changes in your thoughts as well as your actions would be necessary for you to truly be considered "a slave of Christ"?
2. Express how the attitudes of the two types of slaves would differ.

Application Idea

What are some practical actions and attitudes that would convey to others that you are a slave to Christ?

"Don't work only while being watched, in order to please men, but as slaves of Christ, do God's will from your heart."
Ephesians 6:6

2Consider it a great joy, my brothers, whenever you experience vari-
ous trials, 3knowing that the testing of your faith produces endur-
ance. 4But endurance must do its complete work, so that you may
be mature and complete, lacking nothing.

II. Trials Provide Opportunities (1:2-4)

When you read a personal letter, you normally expect the author to make an attempt to express warm and friendly feelings. Then if there were an issue to pursue, he or she would ease into the subject. James launched his message immediately, seemingly dropping a bomb—"Consider it a great joy, my brothers, whenever you experience various trials" (v. 2). In spite of the reference to "trials," he was not throwing out a tough command but a helpful word of encouragement to his "brothers," a term used of both men and women believers, expressing warm affection.

Notes

As children of God, all believers enjoy many rich and meaningful blessings. At the same time we also share difficulties common to all people, such as problems related to health, job, family, and natural disasters. In addition, we can suffer hardships as a result of our relationship to the Lord.

For example, when hardened unbelievers today hear us quote Jesus words, "No one comes to the Father except through Me" (John 14:6), they scream, "Narrow-minded intolerance!" and "Arrogant bigotry!" When we refuse to go along with unethical and immoral business practices, they may label us "not a team player," deny us deserved promotions, and even fire us.

Early Christians faced various forms of persecution by both Jews and Gentiles who were offended by their conviction that Jesus is the one and only way of salvation, by their refusal to worship other gods, and by their stand for righteousness. James knew his readers' faith was being challenged by persecution and difficulties. So he began with encouragement for believers experiencing hard times.

How should we respond when trials come? Usually we say, "Oh no!" James said we should say, "Oh boy!" We should respond with "great joy" (Jas. 1:2). He went on to explain the reason for joy; namely, trials are a means of spiritual growth.

Content Points

1. It has been said that trials can make us bitter, or they can make us better. As we live a life of faith, trials should make us better: from them we should learn, grow, mature, and deepen our faith in God.
2. We should expect trials (or persecution) because of our belief that Jesus is the one and only way of salvation.

Discussion Questions

1. How is it possible to consider it "great joy" to face trials?
2. How do trials often reflect a self-centered attitude focused on comfort and convenience?
3. Have you ever experienced persecution (rejection, taunting, discrimination) because of your faith?

Application Idea

How can we develop these character traits to face trials with "great joy"?

- patience
- perseverance
- wisdom
- faith
- humility
- brotherly love

Pay attention to the reasoning in the following verses. "Trials" translates a word used of things that put us to the test. In chapter 1 James spoke of two kinds of trials: (1) external tests, such as persecution, and (2) internal tests, such as temptations. The noun translated "trials" is related to the word rendered "tempted" in 1:13, where the meaning clearly is the temptation to sin. When we face trials with the right attitude, they are avenues to a stronger faith; with the wrong attitude, they become temptations to evil.

Should we look for trying circumstances? No. The word for "experience" (v. 2) indicates falling into sufferings and calamities. In other words, we don't seek to find trials; they find us. Our obedience and commitment to Christian truth might plunge us into situations that test or try our faith.

James did not offer examples of such situations but simply said such trials are of many kinds. "Various" in verse 2 translates a word meaning literally "many-colored," thus conveying the idea of a wide variety. Trials result from holding to our faith; they include all the problems we may encounter in this uncertain world.

So James wrote first to encourage believers experiencing severe testing. He wanted us to benefit spiritually from our difficulties. In order to do that we need to understand that problems have a positive aspect and can add value to our lives.

James was not presenting an unproved theory but was writing from experience. The term for "knowing" (v. 3) designates experiential knowledge. James had been through the difficulties his readers faced. He learned by experience that the quality of "endurance" (v. 3) is not simply bestowed on believers at the time of their new birth. Christians learn to endure only by going through testing times.

"Endurance" translates a word that means "patience," "steadfastness," or "fortitude." It describes Christians who remain steadfast in their faith regardless of adversity. When we struggle against difficulties and opposition, we can develop this staying power, this ability to hang in there when we'd rather quit.

"Endurance" is not the ultimate goal, however, but the means of reaching the goal. The goal is to become "mature and complete" (v. 4). Failing for any reason to endure in faith greatly hinders spiritual growth.

"Mature" conveys the idea of being fully developed in character and spiritual understanding. "Complete" is a kindred term that means "whole in all its parts." James wanted his readers to have all the spiritual qualities that contribute to a strong Christian character. In other words, God's ultimate purpose is for us to mature, to grow up, to think, act, and react as Jesus did.

Jesus faced the same kinds of problems that we do. Even a brief look at the Gospels shows us that Jesus experienced temptation, loneliness, fatigue, and discouragement. As we go through what Jesus went through, God is working to make us like Jesus. Of course absolute, full maturity will

"Until we all reach unity in the faith and in the knowledge of God's Son, growing into a mature man with a stature measured by Christ's fullness."
Ephesians 4:13

Notes

What character qualities do you lack that keep you from being spiritually complete (mature)?

come only at the end time when God has achieved all His purposes in history. Until that moment James's words exhort us to endure trials so we can grow toward maturity.

"Lacking nothing" emphasizes James's point and guides our attention to the next subject: gaining wisdom to know how to deal properly with trials in the Christian life.

Content Points

1. The trials of which James spoke can be external—such as persecution or difficulties in life—or internal—such as temptation.
2. The Christian character of endurance (patience, perseverance) can only be learned by going through trying times.
3. Endurance is not the goal, but the means to the goal of Christian maturity (v. 4).

Discussion Questions

1. Have you seen your walk with God grow stronger as you relied on Him to resist temptation? How?
2. Can you recall a time of trial in your life that helped you grow and mature as a result of your endurance?
3. Can you think of a trial (difficult circumstance) you did not handle well? What would you do differently?

Application Ideas

1. If maturity requires endurance and endurance requires trials, then we should understand when troubles come our way. Yet if we are honest with ourselves, do we really want to attain maturity?
2. Many would rather settle for partial growth and skip the trials. Without trials, what would we miss?
3. Think about your life circumstances and the situations you are likely to face this week. How can reliance on God help your reactions to be more mature than previous reactions? Pray for God's strength and wisdom as you anticipate facing trials.

[5]Now if any of you lacks wisdom, he should ask God, who gives to
all generously and without criticizing, and it will be given to him.
[6]But let him ask in faith without doubting. For the doubter is like
the surging sea, driven and tossed by the wind. [7]That person should
not expect to receive anything from the Lord. [8]An indecisive man is
unstable in all his ways.

III. *Trials Require Wisdom* (1:5-8)

We instinctively pray when we have difficulty handling a problem. Most of us, however, pray for a quick resolution of the problem. James said we should pray for wisdom instead. Why? So we don't waste an opportunity to grow. If we are not paying attention to what God is teaching us in a trying situation, we face the possibility of being told, as He told the children of Israel, to take another lap around the desert.

Wisdom is tied to being "mature and complete, lacking nothing" (v. 4), so James had a word for those of us who lack wisdom (v. 5). The term translated "lacks" is a banking term that means "experiencing a shortage." Few of us would claim to have a surplus of maturity or wisdom. But who among us can admit to a shortage?

James's use of "wisdom" indicates more than simply knowledge or intelligence. God gifts us with spiritual insight, a moral and spiritual quality based on the "fear of the LORD" (Prov. 1:7). Wisdom differs from knowledge. Wisdom makes decisions about life based on the truth God has revealed to us in Scripture.

Wisdom means godly knowledge put into practice. It gives us the ability to make decisions the way the Lord would make those decisions. Thus to pray for wisdom is to pray for the ability to see all of life—particularly a current troublesome situation—from God's point of view.

What a difference that change of perspective will bring! This gift of wisdom helps us understand the nature and purpose of trials and enables us to grow through enduring them. Without divine wisdom, our natural reaction to hard times could be distress, grief, perplexity, confusion, disappointment, or hopelessness.

While the context relates wisdom to handling trials, let's acknowledge we also can ask for divine wisdom in all of life's circumstances. We need wisdom in relating to the people with whom we live and work, in making decisions that affect our futures and our families, and in ministering and witnessing to others.

"The fear of the LORD is the beginning of knowledge; fools despise wisdom and instruction." Proverbs 1:7

Content Points

1. We should pray for wisdom to face our problems so that we don't lose opportunities to grow.
2. When endurance has made us "mature and complete, lacking nothing", we will have godly wisdom in practice.

Discussion Questions

1. Why did James say to pray for wisdom?
2. What is the difference in wisdom and knowledge?
3. How does wisdom help us understand our trials?
4. If wisdom is making decisions about life based on the truth God has revealed to us in Scripture, how well grounded are you in God's Word?

Notes

Read Luke 18:1-8. Are we as prayerfully persistent as the widow Jesus talked about? Why or why not?

Application Ideas

1. What are some things about which you need to pray for wisdom?
2. Consider the statement "wisdom is godly knowledge put into practice." Do you have difficulty acting on what you know you should do?
3. What steps would move you from knowledge to application?

Trials do not give us wisdom. We receive it as a gift in response to our asking God for it (Jas. 1:5). He will give us the wisdom we need to profit from each trial. The present tense of "ask" signals repeated action, that is, "keep on asking." We gain access to the wisdom we need to meet life's trials by a consistent pattern of prayer.

The fact that God is One who "gives" (v. 5) motivates us to pray. Giving characterizes His nature. He "gives to all generously and without criticizing" (v. 5). We need not fear that we ask God too often for His guidance. He does not reproach, scold, or ignore us when we ask. He gives without restrictions or bargaining. He does not demand detailed explanations. He does not send away sincere petitioners empty-handed.

The words "it will be given to him" (v. 5) are a powerful encouragement for us to pray for wisdom. These words speak of absolute certainty. God willingly hears and answers believers' prayers for wisdom.

The promise about God's answering prayers is limited, however, to those who "ask in faith" (v. 6). This "faith" is not simply an acceptance of certain doctrines about God. It is an active trust, a working faith in God's good will, power, and faithfulness. Thus faith is "without doubting" (v. 6), literally "nothing doubting."

"Doubting" in this context is not skepticism about God's existence. It reveals uncertainty about what kind of God He is. He either keeps His promises or He does not keep them. People who doubt have divided minds and waver between belief and disbelief, trust and distrust. They think prayer might help, but they are reluctant to put much stock in it.

Praying with an attitude of doubt kills effective prayer. It dishonors and insults God by discounting the truth of His promises. Doubt implies that He either is powerless, uncaring, or unreliable.

James pictured doubters as having the same instability as a wave of the sea, blown and tossed by the wind. He compared those who doubt to "the surging sea" on a windy day (v. 6). The picture is not of a wave moving steadily to shore in procession with others but of a choppy wave being blown first one way and then another. The imagery points to vacillation and instability.

Commercial fishermen who spend their lives on the ocean understand the picture James was painting in verse 6. On windy days, the waves rock the boat so that if one is not careful, he will be thrown from one side of the boat to the other. Our attitude in prayer can be like that, first on the faith side, then thrown to the doubting side. The seasoned fisherman learns how to walk the deck, sure-footed against the forces that would toss him. So must we learn to pray and live in faith.

The word "that" (v. 7) is emphatic—"*That* person!" The person in view is, of course, the doubter, one who asks for wisdom with the mouth but does not trust God with the heart. Such people are walking contradictions. With a strong imperative, James told doubters not even to think their prayers would bring "anything from the Lord" (v. 7). Of course this admonition did not mean the loving Father would not bless them at all but that their prayers for wisdom or anything else would not be answered.

James called someone who wavered in this manner "indecisive" (Jas 1:8). The Greek word for "indecisive" literally describes one who has two souls or minds. In this context, the "double-minded" (KJV) or indecisive person is a believer whose Christian life is marred by persistent doubt. This person sorely needs wisdom but could receive it only from God, who does not answer prayers wrapped in doubt. In trying times such believers tend to walk by sight, not by faith.

These indecisive believers are "unstable" (v. 8) in everything, not just in their praying. They have a "yes, but" mentality. They want their own will and God's will at the same time, so they waver between doing evil and doing good. They do not make firm moral choices. These Christians sing "Onward Christian Soldiers" on Sunday but go AWOL (absent without leave) on Monday. Such instability can make them ineffective in every area of life.

Christians certainly may express feelings of inadequacy concerning their faith, as did the father who cried to Jesus—"I do believe! Help my unbelief!" (Mark 9:24). He was not wavering between belief and unbelief but requesting help in believing that Jesus would intervene and a miracle occur.

Content Points

1. Faith (v. 6) is not simply an acceptance of certain doctrines about God. It is an active trust, a working faith in God's good will, power, and faithfulness.
2. Doubting is not skepticism about God's existence; it is uncertainty about what kind of God He is. He either keeps His promises or He doesn't keep them.
3. Praying with an attitude of doubt kills effective prayer, dishonoring and insulting God by discounting the

"We walk by faith, not by sight."
2 Corinthians 5:7

Notes

truth of His promises. It implies that He either is powerless, uncaring, or unreliable.

Discussion Question

1. Why do you think it is necessary to "keep on asking"?
2. When you pray, do you truly believe that God will answer you? Do you put time limits on His answer?

Application Idea

This week, as you pray, remind yourself of what God is: powerful, caring, reliable. As you are reminded of the faithfulness of God, pray believing, not doubting, that your prayers will be answered.

IV. Trials Can Be Financial (1:9-12)

James wrote about two specific kinds of trials related to one's financial situation. He points to the blessing that comes from enduring either or both of them.

[9]The brother of humble circumstances should boast in his exaltation

A. **The Trial of Poverty** (1:9)—Evidently great differences in economic status existed among the members of the early church. Probably the largest number of believers lived essentially a hand-to-mouth existence.

To be in "humble circumstances" (v. 9) describes poverty or a low social standing. "Humble" means "lowly, insignificant weak, or poor," all terms relevant to economically deprived people. James did not rebuke the poor believers for laziness or poor stewardship, so we may assume he was addressing hard-working folk who nonetheless were barely able to make ends meet. He understood how easily they could sink into a swamp of anxiety, depression, bitterness, and resentment.

"Whoever exalts himself will be humbled, and whoever humbles himself will be exalted." Matthew 23:12

James exhorted the poor believers to meet the trial of poverty by boasting in their "exaltation" (v. 9). The word translated "boast" refers to a "joy outwardly expressed as well as inwardly felt." The idea is that poor believers are to focus on their exalted spiritual position in Christ. God has made them new creatures in Christ and has chosen them to be members of His family.

Although the poor may have a low place in earthly society, they can rejoice in their high place as citizens of heaven and heirs of the King of kings. Whatever society thinks about them, the only One who matters holds them in the highest possible esteem. Virtually penniless in this world, they have an eternal wealth beyond calculation waiting for them.

Whether rich or poor, each of us has been placed in the body of Christ to fulfill a role and purpose vital to the work of the church. James's high opinion of poor believers is seen by his use of the tender term for them—"brother"—a word he did not use in speaking to the "rich" in the next verse.

The Lord wants all of us to view ourselves as He views us. The value He places on us and the love He has for us is demonstrated by the cross. Rejoice in the esteem in which the Lord holds us, the grace for living He provides us, and the promises He has given us!

Content Points

1. God's viewpoint toward all people does not depend on their financial circumstances on earth.
2. All believers are "brothers" in Christ.

Discussion Questions

1. How are we still guilty of treating people differently based on background, financial status, race, and poverty? How can we break these habits?
2. In 2 Corinthians 6:10, Paul described himself as "having nothing yet possessing everything." What did he mean? How might his words apply to us?

Application Ideas

1. How can you act differently (biblically) toward those who are in different circumstances than you?
2. What lifestyle patterns do you need to reprioritize?

"Man does not see what the LORD sees, for man sees what is visible, but the LORD sees the heart." 1 Samuel 16:7

[10]But the one who is rich should boast in his humiliation, because he will pass away like a flower of the field. [11]For the sun rises with its scorching heat and dries up the grass; its flower falls off, and its beautiful appearance is destroyed. In the same way, the rich man will wither away while pursuing his activities.

B. The Trial of Wealth (1:10-11)—James warned that the "one who is rich" (v. 10) also would face an economic test of faith. The term "rich" is, of course, a relative term. For many of us, being rich means being economically independent and able to afford a luxurious lifestyle. Most of the world's population, however, would describe the vast majority of North American citizens as rich because they have money beyond that needed to meet life's basic needs.

The test of faith for the financially secure differs from that faced by the poor. The rich are more likely to assume an attitude of superiority and self-sufficiency because of their wealth. If the poor in the churches needed a new view of themselves, so did the few rich people in the fellowship.

James encouraged wealthy believers to take pride in their "humiliation" (v. 10), not in their wealth. James was calling

Notes

them to acknowledge the humiliation of being simply sinners saved by grace. Accordingly, they were to humble themselves before God, being careful at every point to trust in Him, not in their wealth. This attitude would enable them to relate humbly to their fellow brothers and sisters in Christ.

Material wealth can give people a false sense of security. The poor, in their scramble to put food on the table, are constantly reminded of their mortality; the rich, in their comfort, easily might forget that everything in this world, including their lives, is passing away.

James emphasized the mortality of wealthy people by comparing them to fields of lush grass and flowers. Under the blazing and blistering heat of the Middle Eastern sun and the hot southeast winds blowing from the desert (the sirocco), vegetation quickly withers. Human life can disappear just as quickly. One day a wealthy man is "pursuing his activities" (v. 11), cutting deals and making profits, when abruptly his life ends.

Wealthy believers who keep in mind the brevity of life are more likely to view material wealth in its proper perspective. No longer will they give priority to riches and feeding the insatiable desire to make more money. They will find strength in the Lord to resist the sins of trusting in riches and of exalting themselves over others. Instead they will find glory, joy, and satisfaction in what is eternal, including their fellow brothers and sisters in Christ, rather than in what is transitory.

"Then He told them a parable: 'A rich man's land was very productive. He thought to himself, "What should I do, since I don't have anywhere to store my crops? I will do this," he said. "I'll tear down my barns and build bigger ones, and store all my grain and my goods there. Then I'll say to myself, 'You have many goods stored up for many years. Take it easy; eat, drink, and enjoy yourself.'" But God said to him, 'You fool! This very night your life is demanded of you. And the things you have prepared—whose will they be?' That's how it is with the one who stores up treasure for himself and is not rich toward God." Luke 12:16-21

Content Points

1. The rich are "sinners saved by grace," just like the poor.
2. The rich must learn to trust in God, not in their wealth.

Discussion Questions

1. In what ways does wealth test a person spiritually?
2. Read Luke 12:16-21. What warning did Jesus give about trusting in material things?
3. If the rich man is humbled before God and the poor man is exalted, what does that tell us about our priorities in life?

Application Idea

You probably don't consider yourself "rich," but few in the U.S. and Canada can escape the constant lure of materialism and the desire for more. What steps might you take to depend more on God and less on things?

12 Blessed is a man who endures trials, because when he passes the test he will receive the crown of life that He has promised to those who love Him.

C. The Payoff of Enduring Trials (1:12)—Economic or otherwise, trials are tough. Therefore the temptation to "go with the flow" can at times be especially strong. Why should we hang in there? Why not take the easy way out? Is suffering through the struggle worthwhile?

James indicated that enduring trials with faith is more than worth the cost. As he began to conclude the discussion on trials, he again stressed the blessing that belongs to believers who remain faithful.

Already he had explained how trials provide opportunities to endure and thus to grow in faith and character (vv. 2-4). He had pointed out the availability of God's wisdom for coping with trials, particularly the trials posed by poverty and wealth. In verse 12 he apparently used the term "blessed" to summarize the "joy" of verse 2. "Blessed" means "fortunate" or "to be congratulated." Jesus used the same word in the Beatitudes (Matt. 5:3-12).

The blessing for enduring is "the crown of life," literally "the crown which is life" (Jas. 1:12). This term captures both the "joy" (v. 2) and the blessing (v. 12) that belong to believers who remain faithful under trials. While some view this "crown" as eternal life, the context seems to favor a parallel meaning with "mature and complete, lacking nothing" (v. 4).

After all, every believer has eternal life, but the crown of life to which James referred is reserved for those who endure their trials. The Lord wants this life "in abundance" for His people (John 10:10), not only abundance of quantity but also abundance of quality.

What great joy belongs to those who have grown in maturity and thus are able to see life's difficulties and hard knocks from God's perspective and can meet them with God's wisdom and strength! They are the believers who neither gave in to the pressures nor gave up on God, thus passing "the test" (Jas. 1:12). "Test" translates a word that describes testing precious metals and coins to find out if they are genuine.

Hebrews 11 recounts the stories of biblical heroes who kept the faith—kept on believing—when their prayers were not answered during their lifetimes. The test of time has proven the virtue of their endurance. They walked by faith rather than by having to be shown a promising outcome.

By enduring trials, we demonstrate the genuineness of our faith in the Lord and our love for Him, and we receive as our reward the blessing of a higher quality of life.

"For a short time you have had to be distressed by various trials so that the genuineness of your faith—more valuable than gold, which perishes though refined by fire—may result in praise, glory, and honor at the revelation of Jesus Christ." 1 Peter 1:6-7

Content Points

Compare James 1:12 with 1 Peter 1:6-7:

James said we will be rewarded with the "crown of life".	Peter said we will also receive praise, glory, and honor.

Notes

James's phrase "pass the test" speaks of refining metal to prove its genuineness.

Peter said that as fire purifies gold, trials prove the genuineness of our faith.

James and Peter both spoke of reward, good, and hope to come out of our trials.

Discussioin Questioins

1. Name ways James said we are blessed by enduring trials.
2. Can you consider times in your life when you were going through a "trial" and see how your response reflected your faith or lack of faith?
3. Does knowing that God has something good in store for you at the end of the trial(s) help you to endure the trial(s)?

Application Idea

Make a list of each of the following:

1. Ways God can work in your life through trials
2. Promises God has made to see you through the trials
3. Blessings in store for you as you endure trials. Keep these lists and use them to remind and encourage you the next time you face a trial.

[13]No one undergoing a trial should say, "I am being tempted by
God." For God is not tempted by evil, and He Himself doesn't tempt
anyone. [14]But each person is tempted when he is drawn away and
enticed by his own evil desires. [15]Then after desire has conceived, it
gives birth to sin, and when sin is fully grown, it gives birth to death.
[16]Don't be deceived, my dearly loved brothers. [17]Every generous act
and every perfect gift is from above, coming down from the Father
of lights; with Him there is no variation or shadow cast by turning.
[18]By His own choice, He gave us a new birth by the message of truth
so that we would be the firstfruits of His creatures.

V. Temptations Can Be Overcome (1:13-18)

An exasperated man abandoned his car in a no-parking zone and left this note on the windshield: "I've circled this block 20 times. I have an appointment I must keep or lose my job. 'Forgive us our trespasses.' " The man returned from his appointment and found a note from the traffic officer. It read: "I've circled this block for 20 years. If I don't give you a ticket, I'll lose my job. 'Lead us not into temptation.' "

We often make jokes about temptation, but verses 13-18 show that this subject is deadly serious. The Greek words translated "trial" and "temptation" have the same root. The context determines which definition is meant. We endure trials, for God will use them to help us grow up in our faith. We resist temptations, for they are designed to lead us into sin and its dire consequences. We may say that Satan tempts us to bring out the worst in us, but God tests us to bring out the best in us.

James's purpose was not to give a complete analysis of temptation, so he did not mention Satan's role here, though he did in 4:7. Neither did James mention the influential roles of heredity and environment. Instead he described the personal process of temptation to stress the vital need for us to take personal responsibility for our temptations and for how we handle them.

Satan tempts us to bring out the worst in us, but God tests us to bring out the best in us.

How does the notion of being responsible for your temptations grab you? Many of us have assumed temptations just crash in on us. We often blame our temptations on other people, situations, or contemporary culture.

James cut through all the clutter and exposed what lies beneath it: We blame God. Think about that. We justify verbal and physical abuse by saying "I have a temper," which really means "Don't blame me; God made me this way."

We rationalize other sins in a similar way. "I have this strong sex drive" relieves our guilt for immorality. "I have this driving ambition" substitutes for ethical practices. "I have to work with ungodly associates" gets the blame for an ungodly lifestyle. Is this not a subtle way of blaming God for our temptations? "He made me this way and put me where I am, so I can't help it."

This excuse is as old as Adam (see Gen. 3:12). He blamed God for his eating the forbidden fruit because God created Eve. Today we haven't improved on Adam's approach. James blew away this faulty thinking by stating bluntly, "No one undergoing a trial should say, 'I am being tempted by God' " (Jas. 1:13). James's message tells us to wake up and smell the coffee. God has nothing to do with evil. He hates all sin, so He "is not tempted by evil" (v. 13).

"Then the man replied, 'The woman You gave to be with me—she gave me some fruit from the tree, and I ate.'"
Genesis 3:12

People have in their nature an inclination to sin, but God does not. His perfect holiness and righteousness make Him incapable of being tempted; He will never do wrong, nor will He ever wrong us. "He Himself doesn't tempt anyone" (v. 13). Although our temptations are not from God, He allows people to be tested (for example, Abraham and Job), He does not test us with evil purposes. God uses trials to develop Christian character.

God's Word is clear: We alone ultimately are responsible for our temptations. How so? Regardless of outside factors or forces, the immediate source of temptation is our own "evil desires" (v. 14). Our temptations do not lie in any person, object, or outside circumstance. Instead, they stem from within us, from our sinful human nature.

Notes

We have to make a choice when an evil desire flits across our consciousness. We choose either to turn away from it, avoiding temptation, or to turn toward it, inviting temptation. *We choose* self-sacrifice or self-indulgence. *We choose* to reject or to embrace.

"Enticed" (v. 14) describes the act of using bait to hook a fish or to lure an animal into a camouflaged trap. Turning toward the enticing bait rather than away from it results in disastrous consequences. In other words, an evil desire attracts our attention; if we dwell on the possibility of satisfying that evil desire with a sinful thought, word, or deed we have been drawn to sin.

James shifted from the language of fishing/hunting to that of childbirth (v. 15). The Greek words for "desire" and "sin" are both feminine in gender. Therefore we could say that when we give freedom to "evil desire," she comes back from her adventure pregnant ("conceived"). Notice that "sin" is conceived within us before it ever overtly appears. Usually, long before the act of sin is committed on the outside, the intent to sin is established on the inside.

Desire's child turns out to be the "sin," but that's not the end of the matter. Sin develops until it "is fully grown," that is, brought to maturity and ready to give birth itself. Sin's maturity refers to the growth of its strength in controlling us. In the end, its control becomes absolute and thereby self-destructive: Sin "gives birth to death."

This does not mean believers are doomed to hell for their sins. The Bible teaches that we are all sinners by nature and that all sins can be forgiven; however, all sins have consequences. While our sins do not remove us from God's family, sins not confessed and unrepented remove us from His fellowship and useful service. He is the source of all that is good in life; therefore, sin kills the most valuable and significant aspects of life for us believers.

Sin not only disrupts our relationship with God but it also our closest relationships with people. It destroys reputations. It robs us of joy and plunges us into despair. It takes us off life's lovely highways and onto shabby dead-end streets. Thus God warns us not to be fooled by the attractive and enticing appearance of evil. Its promises of delight are lies; it is deadly; it destroys.

CONTENT POINTS

1. God is holy, just, and righteous. He will never tempt us to sin.
2. We alone are ultimately responsible for our temptations. The immediate source of temptation is our own "evil desires" (v. 14). Our temptations stem from our own sinful human nature.

3. For the Christian, sin disrupts our relationship with God as well as our relationships with people.

DISCUSSION QUESTIONS

1. Temptation is like bait in a trap? Compare what happens when the animal takes the bait to what happens when we follow our temptations.
2. What are ways our relationship to God is affected by sin? What are ways that our relationships with others affected by sin?

APPLICATION IDEAS

1. What excuses do you use for your sin? Are you willing to take personal responsibility for your sin? If you don't understand why any excuse is not valid, will you discuss this issue with a mature Christian?
2. How does temptation move from conception to maturity? Use this analogy: Is it easier to fight off a 1,000-pound grizzly bear or a 50-pound cub?
3. Think of another related analogy to share with your group.

Does "Don't be deceived" (v. 16) relate to the deceptive nature of evil desires in the last three verses? Or does it relate more to the mistaken idea that God is the source of the trouble brought on by temptation, sin, and death?

Either interpretation is possible and valid, but verses 16-18 stress further the goodness of God. Perhaps these verses are directed primarily against the idea that God tempts people to sin.

The tender term "my dearly beloved brothers" (v. 16) shows urgent concern. It also softens the plea that readers not "be deceived" in this vital matter. God does not tempt people; we are responsible for our sins.

James stated almost poetically the two-sided truth he wanted his readers to know. **First,** he wanted us to know that God is the source of all good gifts. He declared, "Every generous act and every perfect gift is from above" (v. 17).

A literal reading could be "Every good thing given and every perfect gift is from God." The "generous act" (good thing) refers to the manner in which God gives His gifts. The "perfect gift" refers to the resulting perfection of these gifts. God's gifts are perfect because they fulfill His will for His people. "From above, coming down" means these good gifts come from God. "The Father of lights" designates the Creator of the universe with all of its lights—sun, moon, and stars.

Second, James assured us that God does not and cannot change. The Greek text for "shadow cast by turning" suggests the shifting shadows cast by earthly objects—the sun or moon—as they move across the sky. Our perception

Notes

of sunlight's intensity changes because of the time of day, clouds, seasons, or eclipses. Moonlight is affected by phases of the moon, clouds, and eclipses as well. So to us the light from sun and moon seems to change from time to time.

God is "the Father of lights" who never changes at all. His love and benevolence toward us do not wax and wane but are constant. God continually gives only good gifts to His children, and genuinely good gifts come only from God! God's greatest "generous act" and "perfect gift" to His people is salvation, the new birth (see John 3:3-21).

James made three observations about this new birth. **First**, "By His own choice, He gave us a new birth" (Jas. 1:18). He acted by His will, freely with no outside influence. God's will does not include luring us to sin but giving us new life in Christ. **Second,** God gives this new birth by the message of truth, that is, "the gospel of salvation" (Eph. 1:13). James was referring to a spiritual rather than natural or physical birth.

Third, James identified the purpose of this new birth—"that we would be the firstfruits of His creatures" (Jas. 1:18). In the Old Testament *firstfruits* refer to the first portion of the harvest, which was given as an offering to God.

The Christians in James's day represented the firstfruits of God's new redeemed people in Jesus Christ. God puts His heart into giving us life worth living now and forever. Trials will continue to come to us in all shapes and sizes. Remain faithful by asking God for wisdom and trusting His goodness.

Content Points

1. God is the source of everything good in life (good gifts).
2. God does not change. His nature and promises today will be His nature and promises tomorrow.
3. God's greatest gift is salvation through Jesus Christ.

Discussion Questions

1. Do we often take the good things in life for granted? How can we develop the habit of gratefulness?
2. James 1:17 reads, "With Him there is no variation or shadow cast by turning." How does this verse affect your faith in God?

Application Ideas

1. Too often we blame God for what goes wrong. In verses 5-8, what did James say might be the problem?
2. What are some things for which you need to stop blaming God?
3. How can you develop an "attitude of gratitude" ?

"Give thanks in everything, for this is God's will for you in Christ Jesus."
1 Thessalonians 5:18

SUMMARY

1. James, the half brother of Jesus, wrote to the Jewish and Gentile believers who through persecution were now living in all parts of the Roman Empire.

2. The Christian character of endurance (patience, perseverance) can only be learned by experiencing trials.

3. All Christians need wisdom, which is godly knowledge put into practice. Praying with an attitude of doubt kills effective prayer, dishonors and insults God, and implies He either is powerless, uncaring, or unreliable.

4. The trial of poverty can sink people into a swamp of anxiety, depression, bitterness, and resentment. The trial of wealth can give rich people a false sense of security and an attitude of superiority and self-sufficiency.

5. Faith (v. 6) is an active trust in God's good will, power, and faithfulness. God will never tempt us to sin. The source of temptation is our own "evil desires" (v. 14).

8 An indecisive man is unstable in all his ways.

Going Deeper—Indecisive

Authentic, vibrant Christianity depends on our living moment-by-moment in the reality of knowing Jesus Christ. That knowledge comes through making a faith commitment to Him. The term indecisive or, more literally, double-minded, describes people with divided loyalties in heart and mind.

They attempt to serve both God and self, both the spirit and the body, both light and darkness, both heavenly wisdom and human wisdom. They pray, but their prayers are not genuine. They step out in faith, but then step back. They seek spiritual answers from God's Word but explain them away with human wisdom. Such indecisiveness lies behind the hot-and-cold instability of some Christians.

JAMES 1:19-27 (HCSB)

[19]My dearly loved brothers, understand this: everyone must be
quick to hear, slow to speak, and slow to anger,
[20]for man's anger does not accomplish God's righteousness.
[21]Therefore, ridding yourselves of all moral filth and evil excess,
humbly receive the implanted word, which is able to save you.
[22]But be doers of the word and not hearers only, deceiving your-
selves. [23]Because if anyone is a hearer of the word and not a doer,
he is like a man looking at his own face in a mirror; [24]for he looks
at himself, goes away, and right away forgets what kind of man
he was. [25]But the one who looks intently into the perfect law of
freedom and perseveres in it, and is not a forgetful hearer but a
doer who acts—this person will be blessed in what he does. [26]If
anyone thinks he is religious, without controlling his tongue but
deceiving his heart, his religion is useless. [27]Pure and undefiled
religion before our God and Father is this: to look after orphans
and widows in their distress and to keep oneself unstained by
the world.

Unit One: Grow Up!

Lesson Two

EXAMINE YOUR LIFE BY GOD'S WORD (JAMES 1:19-27)

I. **Prepare to Hear God's Word (1:19-21)**

II. **Respond to God's Word (1:22-27)**

A. The Instruction: Be Doers of the Word (v. 22)

B. The Illustration: Look in the Mirror (vv. 23-25)

C. The Application: Practice What You Profess (vv. 26-27)

LEARNING GOALS

As a result of studying this lesson, learners will:

- *Explain the meaning of "the implanted word"*
- *Describe five steps we can take to prepare ourselves to receive God's Word*
- *Cite ways we might deceive ourselves about not obeying the Word*
- *Understand the mirror illustration in James 1:23-25*
- *Evaluate the extent to which our religion pleases God*

Notes

"And you also were included in Christ when you heard the word of truth, the gospel of your salvation."
Ephesians 1:13, NIV

A missionary told about working in New Mexico several years ago. Once he took some Navajo children to see a western movie. A scene near the end portrayed Indians' surrendering to white men. The Indians spoke in Navajo, but English subtitles translated their words as a beautiful speech of surrender and submission. The Navajo children laughed their heads off. They knew the Indians really had said, "You white men are so low you can walk under a snake's belly and not knock off your tall hat."

How well do our lives translate God's Word into what we claim to believe? James 1:19-27 speaks to the inconsistency between proclaimed belief and expressed behavior, between profession and performance. As you study this Scripture passage, see how well your attitudes and actions measure up to God's Word.

[19]My dearly loved brothers, understand this: everyone must be quick to hear, slow to speak, and slow to anger, [20]for man's anger does not accomplish God's righteousness. [21]Therefore, ridding yourselves of all moral filth and evil excess, humbly receive the implanted word, which is able to save you.

I. *Prepare to Hear God's Word* (1:19-21)

Before we get into a detailed analysis of these verses, we need to determine what James meant by "the implanted word" in 1:21. He could not have meant the New Testament since it was formalized many years after the time of James. The "word" more than likely signified the gospel, the good news about Jesus Christ.

In James's day the truth about Jesus' identity, teachings, and salvation was delivered primarily by word of mouth. It included the message preached either by trusted apostles or by others who had seen and heard Jesus. It might have included recollections of Jesus' preaching and teaching. In worship services the gospel could have been read aloud from some generally accepted documents.

Perhaps this "word" also included a Christian interpretation of passages in the Torah (the name given the first five books of the Old Testament), a reading from which was customary in synagogue services. In our day the gospel truths are recorded in the Bible, all parts of which bear witness to Christ (see Luke 24:27), so we rightly can understand "the implanted word" as meaning for us God's Word.

We also need to acknowledge that James 1:19-21 have been taken two ways, both of which express biblical truth validated elsewhere in the Scriptures.

First, some see the admonition to "be quick to hear, slow to speak, and slow to anger" (v. 19) as counsel about personal relationships. Listening to what people have to say shows our interest in them and expresses Christian love. Being "slow to speak" could mean allowing others to have their full say, or it could indicate measuring our words before speaking them.

Case Study
Read the following. In the margin list possible answers. You will find other suggested answers on page 36.

Barbara told Keith that she thought he was making too many sacrifices to be a deacon. Keith explained that he was being obedient to the commands of Scripture.

Barbara said, "I don't care what the Bible says, I don't think you should."

Barbara let her personal values and priorities take precedence over what God says. How do we make the same mistakes? List ways that you let your own attitudes, desires, priorities, and opinions take priority over the things of God.

"Slow to anger" tells us not to be easily offended or to react unwisely against those who hurt our feelings or work against us. Seething resentment should never characterize a believer. The Lord taught us to forgive one another and to love our enemies and do good to them. Thus "man's anger does not accomplish God's righteousness" (v. 20). "Slow to anger" seems to leave room for righteous indignation (see Mark 3:5 and Eph. 4:26).

For instance, we should be angry about injustice, discrimination, and oppression. Nevertheless, when husbands and wives, parents and children, employees and employers are quick to listen, slow to speak, and slow to become angry, relationships are healthier and stronger.

Second, other Bible scholars view James 1:19-21 as counsel about preparing to "receive the implanted word" (v. 21), and the broader context seems to support this view. James 1:18 speaks of "the message of truth" that results in the "new birth." The paragraph following verses 19-21 stresses living by God's truth. This context seems to relate verses 19-21 primarily to preparing to receive God's message. We rightly expect pastors and teachers to prepare to deliver the truth of God's Word, but let us accept our responsibility for preparing to receive that truth.

Are we willing to admit that all too often we come to worship services or Bible studies unprepared to hear and receive the Word? Have we found ourselves coming, sitting, and waiting for an allotted time to end instead of listening for the voice of God to speak to our hearts through His Word? We need preparation to receive the Word.

Notes

"He who has ears to hear, let him hear."
Matthew 13:9, NKJV

In the margin list possible answers to this question: How can I better prepare myself for the worship services at my church? Other suggested ideas can be found on page 36.

Preparation for any significant task may be more difficult and take more time than the task itself. Whether we are painting a house, cooking a meal, or teaching a Bible study, good preparation is vital for long and lasting results. Likewise, we must be prepared to receive the Word of God if it is to make a difference in the way we live. So what did James have to say about preparing to receive God's Word?

The **first** preparatory step is to "be quick to hear" the Word (v. 19). This kind of hearing means we come not only with open ears but also with open hearts and minds. We come ready to listen and eagerly expecting to hear what God will say to us through His Word.

The **second** step is being "slow to speak" (v. 19), which could refer to new Christians who want to become teachers of God's Word before they understand it themselves. Possibly it refers to our tendency to disagree with biblical truth that cuts against the grain and, so to speak, to talk back to it.

Sometimes God's messages to us are not what we expect. They may call for painful self-sacrifice of some kind. We may say to ourselves or to others, "I don't agree with that" or "Well, I'm not about to do that." We would be better served to slow down and say, "I need to reflect on this truth, pray for God's further enlightenment, and then make whatever adjustments He wants me to make."

The **third** part of preparation to receive God's Word is to be "slow to anger" (v. 19). The Greek word translated "anger" indicates a long-standing resentment. When we fail to forgive people as Scripture teaches, we create spiritual static in our hearts that makes hearing the Word difficult.

Some believers have responded with anger to biblical calls to forgive their enemies. Usually, whether we express the anger or hide it, we direct it at teachers or preachers. Still, if the message is centered in God's Word, our anger actually is directed against God. Can we be angry with God? You bet.

Let's keep in mind the fact that God loves us and wants the best for us. Even when He seems to be denying us our hearts' desires, He works in and through us in ways that lead to greater fruitfulness, fulfillment, and joy. To resent His leadership and disobey His Word is to miss the higher blessings He desires for us in this life.

Even if we obey His Word in a grudging, half-hearted, and resentful way, our anger toward Him will blind us to His love and rob us of some of the richest rewards He desires to give us. The Word of God cannot take root and be fruitful in a heart overrun with resentment.

Even if this anger is only a silent wrath, it still cannot and "does not accomplish God's righteousness" (v. 20). God desires and requires righteous living from His children. That involves hearing His Word with a submissive, teachable spirit.

Content Points

1. The "implanted Word" (v. 21) is the gospel, the message of salvation.
2. Hearing God's Word with our ears is not the same as hearing with our hearts and minds.
3. We need to be "slow to speak" by letting God's Word sink into our minds and hearts before we impulsively respond to it.
4. Anger, resentment, and bitterness toward God will keep His Word from taking root in our hearts.

Discussion Questions

1. Think about your typical Sunday morning experience in Sunday School and worship. What distracts you or keeps you from truly "hearing" God's Word?
2. What can you do to overcome these distractions?
3. Think about your daily lifestyle. What distracts you from spending time in God's Word?

Application Ideas

1. How do you need to prepare yourself to hear God's Word?
2. When you read your Bible or hear a sermon, do you truly expect to hear from God?
3. We profess to believe God's Word, but how do we sometimes reject what it says by our words or actions?
4. Does pride keep you from "hearing" and sometimes being quick to speak, rejecting what God's Word has to say for your life? Pray for the Holy Spirit to help you receive the Word and to apply it.

The **fourth** preparatory step is to get rid of "all moral filth and evil excess" (v. 21). "Filth" describes that which is offensive, repulsive, and disgusting. The term includes sensual sins, though it is not limited to those. The word translated "evil" describes the malignant and malicious desire to see injury inflicted on others. It often refers to hidden sins, motives, and attitudes no one else sees.

"Evil excess" describes evil in the extreme, but James was not indicating that evil in moderation is acceptable. He was using vivid and powerful terms that stress the abhorrent nature of sin. To prepare ourselves to receive what God has to say to us, we must first rid ourselves (literally "strip off") these things.

Notes

To *get clean* we have to *come clean* with God.

"But the one sown on the good ground—this is one who hears and understands the word, who does bear fruit and yields: some 100, some 60, some 30 times what was sown." Matthew 13:23

"Therefore if anyone is in Christ, there is a new creation; old things have passed away, and look, new things have come." 2 Corinthians 5:17

Therefore, to prepare to receive God's words to us, we need to be cleansed from our sins. To *get clean* we have to *come clean* with God. First John 1:9 says, "If we confess our sins, He is faithful and righteous to forgive us our sins and to cleanse us from all unrighteousness." When we confess our sins in the spirit of repentance, we can rely on God to keep His Word and to make us clean in His sight. This is a necessity if we are to be able to hear and heed His Word.

The **fifth** preparatory step is to "humbly receive" God's teachings (Jas. 1:21). This humbling involves an attitude and an action. "Humbly" indicates the right attitude toward the Word. This definition carries the idea of a gentle, open, and teachable spirit. Having this attitude is an essential aspect of being ready to hear God's Word.

"Receive" (v. 21) tells us to do the right thing with what we learn from the Word. The term means "to welcome." We are to welcome the Word of God into our lives, not to argue with it, to resent it, to resist it, or to reject it. We are to receive the Word in total subjection to God's purpose and with a willingness to learn from Him.

As indicated earlier, "the implanted word" (v. 21) is the gospel, but by implication it includes the teachings of the Word of God, the Bible. The term "implanted" (or planted) may be an allusion to the Parable of the Sower, or more precisely, the Parable of the Seed and the Soils (see Matt. 13:3-23). When our hearts are clean and properly prepared, God's truth can take root and produce much fruit.

"Implanted" signifies the gospel already has been welcomed. James was writing to believers. When we receive Christ into our lives by faith, we are saved once and forever. So what do the words "which is able to save you" mean? James most likely was thinking of the climax of our salvation that awaits Jesus's future return.

Two other possible explanations may be offered.

First, those whose lives demonstrate an ongoing openness and obedience to God's Word give evidence of their salvation. **Second,** by remaining open to the influence of God's teachings, we are saved from living pointless and fruitless lives. Our old ways of life have ended, but our new lives in Christ have just begun. We have a lot to learn, so we need to grow in our understanding of the Lord, His salvation, and His expectations of us.

We also have to learn how to put His teachings into practice. To experience the fullness of salvation we must be prepared to remain open to receive and welcome all that the Lord says to us directly though His Spirit, His Word, and people He chooses to use to impact our lives.

Content Points

1. Unconfessed sin can keep us from hearing what God has to say.
2. We are to "welcome" God's Word to us, even when we're uncomfortable with what it has to say.
3. A teachable spirit evidences an humble, open heart.

Discussion Questions

1. How does sin keep us from receiving and applying God's Word to our lives?
2. Describe a "teachable spirit." Does this describe you?

Application Idea

Do you make it a practice to confess your sin every day? Write out 1 John 1:9 on a small note card. Put it where you will regularly see it and be reminded to confess your sins, doing the following:

1. Take time. Don't rush. True confession takes time for soul searching.
2. Humble yourself.

    "God resists the proud, but gives grace to the humble" (Jas. 4:6).

3. Pray for God to show you your sin. Our hearts are so dark, we are often unaware of our own sin.

    "The heart is more deceitful than anything else and desperately sick—who can understand it?" (Jer. 17:9).

4. Confess your sins individually and specifically, not just a blanket "forgive me my sins."
5. Confess sins of mind and mouth, not just deeds of the hands and feet. Are you harboring bitterness, anger, resentment, or unforgiveness toward someone?

    "All bitterness, anger and wrath, insult and slander must be removed from you, along with all wickedness. And be kind and compassionate to one another, forgiving one another, just as God also forgave you in Christ" (Eph. 4:31-32).

    "For if you forgive people their wrongdoing, your heavenly Father will forgive you as well. But if you don't forgive people, your Father will not forgive your wrongdoing" (Matt. 6:14-15).

6. Have you been gossiping or talking about someone in unproductive ways?

    "No rotten talk should come from your mouth, but only what is good for the building up of someone in need, in order to give grace to those who hear" (Eph. 4:29).

Notes

Possible responses to the case study on page 31:

1. How we spend our money
2. How we use our time
3. Our lifestyle choices
4. Unwillingness to serve in church
5. Justifying bitterness, anger, prejudice, and other attitudes

Possible responses to the question on page 32:

1. Spend time with God through the week, in prayer and in the Word.
   "Draw near to God, and He will draw near to you" (Jas. 4:8).
2. Commit your worries and the anxieties of life to God so that your mind is not cluttered with them.
   "Humble yourselves therefore under the mighty hand of God ... casting all your care upon Him, because He cares about you" (1 Pet. 5:6-7).
3. Discipline yourself to get to bed earlier on Saturday night so that you can have a clear mind on Sunday morning.
4. Make preparations for church on Saturday night:
   Lay out clothes for children and yourself.
   Prepare the baby's diaper bag.
   Get Bible, lesson, and other materials together.
5. As you get up, get ready, and drive to church, don't listen to secular music or TV or read the morning paper. Listen to Christian music or enjoy the silence to be with God.
   "Set your minds on what is above, not on what is on the earth" (Col. 3:2).
6. Make as few commitments as possible for Sunday so that it can truly be a Sabbath day of rest. If you're thinking about your afternoon shopping list or the yard work to do when you get home, you may miss what God is trying to say to you through the "clutter" of life.
   "On the seventh day He rested and was refreshed" (emphasis added) *(Ex. 31:17).*
7. Resolve to leave Monday's worries for Monday.
   "Therefore don't worry about tomorrow, because tomorrow will worry about itself. Each day has enough trouble of its own" (Matt. 6:34).

[22]But be doers of the word and not hearers only, deceiving your-
selves. [23]Because if anyone is a hearer of the word and not a doer, he
is like a man looking at his own face in a mirror; [24]for he looks at
himself, goes away, and right away forgets what kind of man he was.
[25]But the one who looks intently into the perfect law of freedom and
perseveres in it, and is not a forgetful hearer but a doer who acts—
this person will be blessed in what he does. [26]If anyone thinks he is
religious, without controlling his tongue but deceiving his heart, his
religion is useless. [27]Pure and undefiled religion before our God and
Father is this: to look after orphans and widows in their distress and
to keep oneself unstained by the world.

II. *Respond to God's Word* (vv. 22-27)

Just because we have been in church or Bible study and have heard the Word does not mean we are applying what we have heard. Simply agreeing with the Word does not mean we actually are doing what the Word says. James addressed the gross inconsistency in the lives of many professed Christians. He did this by giving instruction, by illustrating the instruction, and by presenting a practical application.

[22]But be doers of the word and not hearers only, deceiving yourselves.

A. The Instruction: Be Doers of the Word (v. 22)—The instruction is to be "doers of the word and not hearers only, deceiving yourselves." In 1:14-16 James zeroed in on our personal responsibility. Yes, Satan has a goal of leading us away from divine truth, and thus Jesus called him the father of liars (John 8:44). Regardless of Satan and all the means he may use to delude us, we are accountable for hearing and obeying God's Word.

Listening regularly to spiritual truth without putting it into practice is a form of self-deception. The use of "yourselves" emphasizes that such deception is our own fault and no one else's. Unfortunately many of us have deceived ourselves into believing that reading the Bible or hearing its message proclaimed is an end in itself.

But James called for action once we have been exposed to Scripture. Being merely a hearer is similar to college students who audit a course. The students are permitted to attend class, listen carefully, and take notes. However, they are not penalized if they skip class. They do not have to do anything outside of class, such as reading, memorizing, or writing reports. They do not take exams. They don't have to think about what they hear in class, fully understand it, or do anything at all about it.

All of us do well to consider whether we are auditing Bible study sessions in Sunday School, sermons in worship services,

"How can a young man keep his way pure? By living according to your word. I have hidden your word in my heart that I might not sin against you."
Psalm 119:9,11, NIV

Notes

and our own Bible reading. We demonstrate authentic faith by applying biblical truth. We show we believe it by living it out in daily life.

Content Points

1. We are accountable for hearing and obeying God's Word.
2. Hearing, reading, or even studying the Bible is self-deception if we do not apply it.
2. Authentic faith is lived out by applying the truth of God's Word.

Discussioin Questions

1. In what ways do we often deceive ourselves into thinking we are doing what God wants?
2. How can people "audit" the Bible?

Application Ideas

Each week, take time on Sunday afternoon or evening to reflect on the sermon and/or Sunday School lesson. Ask yourself, "What difference does this make in my life?" "What do I need to do to apply this truth in a practical way as I relate to others?"

23Because if anyone is a hearer of the word and not a doer, he is like a man looking at his own face in a mirror; 24for he looks at himself, goes away, and right away forgets what kind of man he was. 25But the one who looks intently into the perfect law of freedom and perseveres in it, and is not a forgetful hearer but a doer who acts—this person will be blessed in what he does.

B. The Illustration: Look in the Mirror (vv. 23-25)—James used an illustration to magnify the difference between merely hearing the Word and obeying it. Those who are hearers and not doers act like one who, after "looking at his own face in a mirror," then "goes away, and right away forgets what kind of man he was" (vv. 23-24).

"Looking" translates a word that means "to study carefully and thoroughly, to perceive." Though some disagree, this refers to more than a quick glance on the way out the door. (See **Going Deeper,** p. 46.)

Those who examine their own faces see what they look like, even as their appearances change due to age or life experiences. This examination reveals whether one needs to take some action, such as washing a dirty face or treating a blemish. The folk who are "hearers only" see what changes or improvements the Word reveals they should make in their lives, but they get up and go about business as usual.

They ignore and quickly forget what God's Word showed them. In other words, they saw their sins clearly exposed by the Word, but they chose to forget rather than to repent, to go their own way rather than obey.

How can anyone ignore God's Word and not put it into practice? Remember how easily we can deceive ourselves (v. 22). We might rationalize that everybody falls short and thus minimize to ourselves our own shortcomings—"After all, nobody is perfect." We might focus our thoughts on ways we are obeying other teachings of the Word, thinking our obedience sort of balances or cancels out our disobedience—"I'm a pretty good Christian." We might point to others who fall far shorter than we do and argue that at least we attend church and hear the Word—"Look at my neighbors. They never even darken the door of the church."

"Why do you call Me 'Lord, Lord,' and don't do the things I say?" Luke 6:46

A common way we deceive ourselves is by delaying obedience—"I'll do something about this tomorrow." Worst of all, we may tell ourselves we believe in Jesus as Lord and Savior; therefore, we don't have to be concerned about obedience to the Word. We dare not forget His pointed question, "Why do you call Me 'Lord, Lord,' and don't do the things I say?" (Luke 6:46). Knowing what God's Word tells us to do and ignoring it leads us onto treacherous ground.

"If you love me, you will obey what I command." John 14:15, NIV

James 1:25 presents a contrast to the forgetful and idle hearer of the Word. The person whose example all of us can follow is one who "looks intently into the perfect law of freedom and perseveres in it ... but a doer who acts—this person will be blessed in what he does." James's words are emphatic; those who are doers of the Word receive God's blessing. Fulfilling God's purposes always brings His blessings.

Note the path that leads to blessedness. **First,** the believer who is blessed "looks intently" into God's Word. The verb (not the same as "looks" in v. 23) means "to look closely or seriously." Christians are blessed as they read or listen to the Word, searching eagerly for God's message to them. God's Word provides the standard for living according to God's will.

James described God's Word as the "perfect law of freedom" (v. 25). James was not referring to the law of Moses or the Old Testament. For him, "law" represented the sum total of God's revealed truth. This truth includes the final revelation made through Christ and to the apostles.

As perfect, this law is complete, whereas the law of Moses was only preparatory. This perfect law of the new covenant is energized by the Holy Spirit; it is internal, living, and powerful as opposed to the external code of rules and regulations of the Old Covenant.

"How I love Your teaching! It is my meditation all day long." Psalm 119:97

This law gives spiritual freedom to those who submit to its authority. God's truth about salvation and living enables individuals to find the freedom to become the persons God created them to be and to fulfill His purposes for them.

Notes

Second, blessings belong to believers who regularly study and examine God's Word—those who "persevere in it" (v. 25). This includes meditating on God's truths (see Ps. 1:1-2). **Third,** such believers remember what they hear—they aren't "forgetful hearers." **Fourth,** they practice God's Word—they "act." Obeying God's Word is the pattern of their lifestyles.

James called each one of us to put God's Word into practice. We are to determine what changes Scriptures tell us to make to bring our attitudes and actions in line with God's will. Then we are to rely on His help as we make those changes. The person who lives by the Book gives careful attention to the Scriptures, responds positively, applies what is heard, and enjoys personal fulfillment.

Content Points

1. God's blessing does not come from hearing His Word, but from acting upon it.
2. God's perfect law, His Word, is not about external rules but living, internal principles which bring true life, and thus, freedom.
3. Faithful believers remember what they hear and do it. They live it out.

Discussion Questions

1. What are ways we rationalize or excuse ourselves from obeying God's Word?
2. What are the dangers of not obeying God's Word?
3. In our society, we often view "law" and "freedom" as opposites. How then can Scripture be the "perfect law of freedom"? Isn't that an oxymoron?

Appllication Ideas

In your time with God, as you read His Word, stop and ask yourself these questions:

- Why does this matter to me?
- What application does this have to my life?
- How would my daily life be different if I applied this truth?
- What steps do I need to take to see these principles become a reality in my life?
- How will I let this truth change my behavior or attitude today?

[26]If anyone thinks he is religious, without controlling his tongue but deceiving his heart, his religion is useless. [27]Pure and undefiled religion before our God and Father is this: to look after orphans and widows in their distress and to keep oneself unstained by the world.

C. The Application: Practice What You Profess (vv. 26-27)— James gave a straightforward application of living out the Word in verses 26-27. The real test of our Christian faith is not how often we attend church services, how many notes we take, how much we listen to Christian music, or the many other things we do and say that characterize contemporary church life. The real test comes day by day as we live out our faith in a world that does not know Christ. James identified three specific ways Christians can put God's Word into practice: controlling our speech, showing compassion for the needy, and living pure lives.

Living out our faith involves "controlling" our tongues (v. 26), being careful about what we say and how we say it. The word translated "controlling" literally is "bridling." It pictures a wild horse needing a bit and bridle to bring it under control. Speech also needs discipline and wise restraint.

James knew some people talk one way at church and another out in the world. Such people consider themselves religious because they attend public worship, give offerings, or help others on occasion. These practices, though good, do not necessarily mean these people have genuine faith. If they do not consistently keep a tight rein on their tongues, they show their religion has no value. Careless speech includes slander, sarcasm, criticism, profanity, and lying.

Church members who do not control their tongues deceive themselves. They think their religious observances please God and have convinced themselves they really are religious. Yet their words reveal worldly hearts, showing their religion to be a pretense. That kind of religion is "useless" (v. 26), a term that translates a word meaning "vain, futile, fruitless." Religious practices that have no effect on one's daily life do not please God or positively impact others.

"No rotten talk should come from your mouth, but only what is good for the building up of someone in need, in order to give grace to those who hear."
Ephesians 4:29

A man sent to a church a couple of e-mails that illustrate both a bad and a good use of the tongue. The first e-mail asked whether a particular person was a member of that church. When informed that the individual was part of that congregation, he sent another message under the title "Today I witnessed a Christian in action."

He had been waiting for a large shipment that was several weeks overdue. The trucking company where the church member worked was to make the delivery but was not responsible for the delay. Nonetheless, when the customer finally received the shipment, he was furious.

He wrote, "I had made up my mind that someone was going to get a piece of my mind even before I met your member. I treated him extremely poorly, even though none of the problems were any of his doing. After I had finished complaining and criticizing (or at least paused a bit), he

Notes

"Thoughtless words can wound as deeply as any sword." Proverbs 12:18a, GNT

"A father of the fatherless and a champion of widows is God in His holy dwelling." Psalm 68:5

stated, 'If you don't already have a church home, I'd like you to be my guest at First Baptist Church.'

"This floored me. I instantly realized what a jerk I had been. I do already have a church home, which I attend regularly with my family, but I certainly didn't learn my attitude from my church or my family or from biblical examples.

"Needless to say I felt like dirt. I apologized, but my after-the-fact apology could not possibly have made up for what I put your member through. Despite my attacks, however, he was helpful, positive, and Christlike. I have never seen anything like it. Some of the best people I have known would not have handled this situation with the attitude he expressed.

"I feel it is my responsibility to express my appreciation to your member for his example and for the lesson of the day, if not the lesson of a lifetime. Also I hope that others may also learn from my mistake. I want to express my apology to him along with my sincerest thanks for a much needed lesson."

James would chime in that we should indeed learn from this man's misuse of his tongue and from the excellent example of the church member's controlling his own.

In verse 27, James did not intend to give a complete definition of religion. Instead, he wanted to present some positive evidence of a religion that is real rather than useless. He emphasized that genuine religion does not consist only of carefully observed rituals. True and acceptable religion changes one's life inwardly and shows itself outwardly in loving service to others and holiness before God.

Thus the kind of useful religion that pleases God is "pure and undefiled" (v. 27). The two terms are quite similar in meaning. Perhaps "pure" characterizes the inner quality of the religious person and "undefiled" describes that person's relationships with the outside world.

Note the two examples of pure and undefiled religion. **First** is "to look after orphans and widows in their distress" (v. 27). These two groups were among the most vulnerable in the ancient world, and the Old Testament often mentions God's concern for them (see Ps. 68:5).

The use of "Father" in referring to "God" fits His expectation that we have compassion for needy people. As His children, we are to take a personal interest in those who have needs they cannot meet and help them in ways that are both wise and practical.

Second, a pure and faultless religion includes moral purity. Genuinely religious people keep themselves "unstained by the world" (v. 27). The term "world" in this context represents the total system of evil that opposes God and righteousness. This evil influences every aspect of human life. Believers are to avoid becoming contaminated by the surrounding evil so they can offer themselves as "a living sacrifice, holy and pleasing to God" (Rom. 12:1).

James warned that our religion is worthless unless it leads us to control our tongues, to help others, and to abstain from impure living. We relate to others according to God's Word when we follow these principles.

Content Points

1. Careless speech betrays the shallowness of our faith.
2. True faith changes one's life inwardly and shows itself outwardly in loving service to others and holiness before God.
3. True religion involves:
    - our hearts (purity)
    - our mouths (speech)
    - our hands (actions and service)
4. God is the Father of all, and we are His children.

Discussiion Questions

1. If someone told you that your faith was "vain, futile, and fruitless," would the evidence of your daily speech prove him or her wrong?
2. Think about the everyday conversations that you have with friends on the phone, sitting in the break room at work, at the coffee shop, or in a church hallway. Would you say the same things about others and display the same attitudes if you were talking to your pastor? If you were talking to Jesus?
3. James described true religion as affecting:
    - our hearts (purity)
    - our mouths
    - our hands (actions and service)

   Describe some of the struggles we have with each of these aspects in our lives.
4. How do we justify not helping people?
5. We tend to stereotype "helping others" as giving financially. In what other ways can we help and be a blessing to others?
6. Psalm 101:3 (NLT) says: "I will refuse to look at anything vile and vulgar." What can we do to safeguard our purity in the following areas?
    - watching television and movies
    - surfing the Internet
    - interacting with the opposite sex at work and elsewhere
7. What other temptations test our purity?

"Then the righteous will answer Him, 'Lord, when did we see You hungry and feed You, or thirsty and give You something to drink? When did we see You a stranger and take You in, or without clothes and clothe You? When did we see You sick, or in prison, and visit You?' And the King will answer them, 'I assure you: Whatever you did for one of the least of these brothers of Mine, you did for Me.'" Matthew 25:37-40

Notes

Application Ideas

1. In a popular TV show a character who was known for having a biting tongue resolved to do something about it. He got an electrical shock device, attached it to his body, and told a friend to give him a jolt every time he said something insulting toward others or boastful about himself. If you were to do the same, how often would you be "shocked"? What practical steps can you take to "bridle" your mouth?
2. Think about Ephesians 4:29 (NIV): *"Do not let any unwholesome talk come out of your mouths, but only what is helpful for building others up according to their needs, that it may benefit those who listen."*
   Evaluate your daily speech according to this checklist:
   - Is it wholesome? Does it reflect Christ?
   - Is it helpful? Does it benefit anyone?
   - Does it build someone up or tear someone down?
   - Does it speak to what someone needs to hear? Is it helpful? Is it encouraging?
   - Do listeners benefit from what you are saying? How?

   If our speech can't pass this 5-point test, we need to be quiet.
3. When was the last time (outside the Christmas holiday season) that you went out of your way to help someone in need? Are you aware of someone you could help today in some way? What are you going to do?
4. Look at discussion question #6 on the previous page. What is one specific thing you need to start doing this week to safeguard the purity of your heart and mind? *"Above all else, guard your heart, for it affects everything you do" (Prov. 4:23, NLT).*

SUMMARY

1. The "implanted word" is God's Word, specifically the message of the Gospel.

2. Five steps help prepare us to receive God's Word: (a) "be quick to hear," (b) "slow to speak," (c) "slow to anger," (d) rid of "all moral filth and evil excess," and (d) "humbly receive" God's teachings.

3. We commonly rationalize disobedience by trying to:
   - minimize our shortcomings ("Nobody is perfect.")
   - think our obedience in some areas offsets disobedience in other areas
   - compare ourselves to others who appear "worse" than us

- delaying obedience ("I'll do it tomorrow.")
- thinking that grace excuses disobedience

4. James's analogy of a person looking in a mirror and forgetting what he looks like is comparable to a person who sees his sin and shortcomings in God's Word and then ignores or chooses to forget rather than repent and obey.

5. Our religion is true and pleases God to the extent that it involves:
   - our hearts (purity)
   - our mouths (speech)
   - our hands (actions and service)

[24]For he looks at himself, goes away, and right away forgets what kind of man he was. [25]But the one who looks intently into the perfect law of freedom and perseveres in it, and is not a forgetful hearer but a doer who acts—this person will be blessed in what he does.

Going Deeper—"Looking" and "Looks"

James 1:23-25 uses two different verbs translated "looking" and "looks" in the illustration about a person viewing himself in a mirror. One verb is used in verses 23-24 to describe the one who hears without doing, but another verb is used in verse 25 to describe the one who acts on what he hears.

In verse 23 the present active participle of katanoeo *is translated "looking." This verb is derived from two words: the preposition* kata, *which basically means "down," and the verb* noeo, *which means "to perceive, apprehend, understand, or gain an insight into."*

A. T. Robertson suggested it literally means "to put the mind down on."[1] In verse 24 a form of this same verb is translated "looks." Occasionally, however, this verb might be used in the simple sense of merely "looking" at something.

For example, the ancient Greek translation of the Old Testament, the Septuagint, uses this verb in the phrase "delightful to look at" (Gen. 3:6). Scholars, therefore, do not all agree on its meaning in James 1:23-24. Some think it indicates a casual glance; others think it indicates understanding what one sees. James's point was to contrast hearing the Word and doing nothing about it to hearing the Word and acting on it. Thus to take the verb in its usual sense of understanding something seems best.

The verb translated "looks intently" in verse 25 is parakupto, *which means literally "to bend over to*

Notes

"Do not owe anyone anything, except to love one another, for the one who loves another has fulfilled the law.
The commandments:
Do not commit adultery,
do not murder,
do not steal,
do not covet,
and if there is any other commandment—all are summed up by this: Love your neighbor as yourself. Love does no wrong to a neighbor. Love, therefore, is the fulfillment of the law."
Romans 13:8-10

see something better." Its meaning is "to look closely or seriously." The preposition eis *means "into." These two words clearly communicate looking intently into the Word of God so as to understand fully the significance and implications of what one is seeing in order to put it into practice.*

[25]But the one who looks intently into the perfect law of freedom and perseveres in it, and is not a forgetful hearer but a doer who acts—this person will be blessed in what he does.

Going Deeper—The Perfect Law of Liberty

For the New Testament Christian, the words "law" and "freedom" seem to be contradictory, even antagonistic; thus the phrase "law of freedom" appears to be an oxymoron. It is hard to see the "law" as a "law of freedom."

First, the law is perfect (Ps. 19:7, KJV, NASB, NIV) because it reflects the nature of our perfect, holy God: "Be holy because I, the LORD your God, am holy" (Lev. 19:2).

The purpose of the law is to help man become what he was created to be—holy, as God is holy. The law does not set us right with God for salvation (Rom. 3:28; Eph. 2:8-9); but when properly understood and applied, it leads us into holiness, to live as He has called us to live and to be what He created us to be.

One of Jesus' most ignored statements is "Don't assume that I came to destroy the Law or the Prophets. I did not come to destroy but to fulfill" (Matt. 5:17; cf. 18-20). Jesus came to initiate a covenant which is new, but in which obedience is still foundational: "Look, the days are coming ... when I will make a new covenant ... I will place My law within them and write it on their hearts. I will be their God, and they will be My people" (Jer. 31:31a, 33b; cf. 31-34). Only four verses previously, James had referred to this new covenant law: "humbly receive the implanted word, which is able to save you" (Jas. 1:21).

Jesus still calls His followers to obedience:

> *"If you love Me, you will keep My commandments" (John 14:15).*
> *"The one who has My commands and keeps them is the one who loves Me" (John 14:21)*

The difference in Jesus' new covenant is that the law is no longer something externally imposed upon us but is internal, "implanted" according to James, and "written on our hearts" according to Jeremiah. Thus this perfect law is part of our new nature, enabled by the Holy Spirit. Even though Jesus set a high standard of discipleship, He was able to say, "My yoke is easy and My burden is light" (Matt. 11:30).

So how is this new law a "law of freedom"? Paul connected the two ideas in Galatians 5:13-14: "For you are called to freedom, brothers; only don't use this freedom as an opportunity for the flesh, but serve one another through love. For the entire law is fulfilled in one statement: Love your neighbor as yourself."

The Mosaic law began as a lengthy, detailed list of rules for every area of life and was then expanded beyond measure in the Pharisaical tradition. In this process, the law became a weighty burden that no man was capable of bearing (Luke 11:46). Instead, the new covenant sets us free to follow one overarching principle: love. Love God. Love others (Matt. 22:36-40; Luke 10:25-28). Saint Augustine said that we are to love God with all our heart and do whatever we want to do. Therein is freedom. No longer bound by a laundry list of do's and don'ts. We are free to live in a loving relationship with our Heavenly Father and with each other. (See Rom. 13:8-10.)

In Christ, we are set free from slavery to sin (John 8:34; Romans 6:18); and through the indwelling presence and power of the Holy Spirit (2 Cor. 3:17), we are free to follow Christ in obedience through love (1 John 3:23) as we are transformed into His image (Rom. 8:29; 2 Cor. 3:18). "If you continue in My word, you really are My disciples. You will know the truth, and the truth will set you free" (John 8:31-32). James used the phrase "law of freedom" again in 2:12.

1. A. T. Robertson, *Word Pictures in the New Testament*, Vol. 6, (Broadman Press: Nashville, TN), 23.

JAMES 2:1-13 (HCSB)

[1]My brothers, hold your faith in our glorious Lord Jesus Christ without showing favoritism. [2]For suppose a man comes into your meeting wearing a gold ring, dressed in fine clothes, and a poor man dressed in dirty clothes also comes in. [3]If you look with favor on the man wearing the fine clothes so that you say, "Sit here in a good place," and yet you say to the poor man, "Stand over there," or, "Sit here on the floor by my footstool," [4]haven't you discriminated among yourselves and become judges with evil thoughts?

[5]Listen, my dear brothers: Didn't God choose the poor in this world to be rich in faith and heirs of the kingdom that He has promised to those who love Him? [6]Yet you dishonored that poor man. Don't the rich oppress you and drag you into the courts? [7]Don't they blaspheme the noble name that you bear?

[8]If you really carry out the royal law prescribed in Scripture, Love your neighbor as yourself, you are doing well. [9]But if you show favoritism, you commit sin and are convicted by the law as transgressors. [10]For whoever keeps the entire law, yet fails in one point, is guilty of breaking it all. [11]For He who said, Do not commit adultery, also said, Do not murder. So if you do not commit adultery, but you do murder, you are a lawbreaker.

[12]Speak and act as those who will be judged by the law of freedom. [13]For judgment is without mercy to the one who hasn't shown mercy. Mercy triumphs over judgment.

Lesson Three

TREAT ALL PEOPLE RIGHT (JAMES 2:1-13)

I. The Principle: Don't Show Favoritism (2:1-4)

II. The Problems with Favoritism (2:5-11)

A. Favoritism Is Unreasonable (vv. 5)

B. Favoritism Is Misdirected (vv. 6-7)

C. Favoritism Is Unloving (v. 8)

D. Favoritism Is Unchristian (vv. 9-11)

III. The Prescription for Avoiding Favoritism (vv. 12-13)

A. Live in Light of Judgment (v. 12)

B. Show Mercy (v. 13)

LEARNING GOALS

As a result of studying this lesson, learners will:

- *Define favoritism and cite current examples of favoritism*
- *Offer four reasons why favoritism is wrong for believers*
- *Explain the meaning of "the royal law"*
- *Understand "the law of freedom"*
- *Follow two prescriptions for avoiding favoritism*

Notes

Regardless of who we are or where we are, we do not want others to play favorites—unless, of course, we are the favorite. A child does not want a teacher to play favorites among the students. A teacher doesn't want the principal to play favorites among the faculty. An employee does not want management to play favorites among the workers. No company executive wants a supplier to play favorites among the competition. And no church committee member wants someone on the church staff to play favorites during the budgeting process.

Nevertheless, all of us sometimes favor show favoritism and in the process discriminate. If you claim to be above showing favoritism, think a bit. Do we not have a tendency to respond to others based on their appearance, which leads to showing favor or disfavor? If they look nice, smell nice, dress nice, and talk nice, we typically respond warmly to them. If they are unattractive, dirty, and are asking for assistance, we often brush them off as soon as possible.

Since the 9/11 bombing in New York City, people of Middle Eastern descent in the United States have experienced considerable discrimination. How do you respond to them? Would you invite them to a block party? Ancestry, race, ethnic background, language—all these are factors that may play a role in favoritism.

What about the age factor? Why do you think laws have been passed to curb discrimination against the elderly in the workplace? What is your reaction to an elderly person who drives slower than you think is necessary?

We also tend to evaluate people on the basis of their achievements. Our society gushes over a winner and forgets the loser. One minute he or she is a hero and the next minute a zero.

In short, none of us can exempt ourselves from the temptation to favor some people over others. All of us, therefore, need to hear and ponder what God has revealed through James about treating people in the right way.

1 My brothers, hold your faith in our glorious Lord Jesus Christ
without showing favoritism. 2 For suppose a man comes into your
meeting wearing a gold ring, dressed in fine clothes, and a poor
man dressed in dirty clothes also comes in. 3 If you look with favor
on the man wearing the fine clothes so that you say, "Sit here in a
good place," and yet you say to the poor man, "Stand over there," or,
"Sit here on the floor by my footstool," 4 haven't you discriminated
among yourselves and become judges with evil thoughts?

1. The Principle: Don't Show Favoritism (vv. 1-4)

James recognized both the temptation to favoritism and the travesty of it. If God loved all of us enough to send His Son to die for us, He obviously values every single one of us. God, therefore, expects His people to value one another without favoring some over others.

James began to stress this truth by addressing fellow believers as "my brothers" (2:1). Our Father loves all of His children, so they ought to love their brothers and sisters. They share together "faith in our glorious Lord Jesus Christ" (v. 1). The basis for Christian fellowship and harmony is love. While we may differ in various ways and have diverse preferences, we share a spiritual kinship that trumps all differences. Without exception we should treat one another as precious family members.

In verse 1 "glorious" could be more than a simple adjective describing the Lord Jesus. Possibly it refers to the shining glory of God Himself (see Isa 60:2; Luke 2:9; Rom. 9:4). What a statement! Besides powerfully expressing Jesus' deity, the term reminds us that all human distinctions—such as wealth, rank, and status—are as nothing in His shining presence. We err if we allow those distinctions to govern our response to people.

God's Word thus commands those of us who share faith in Christ to hold our faith "without showing favoritism" (Jas. 2:1). The Greek word for "favoritism" is a compound word that means "to receive" and "face." It literally means "to receive somebody's face," to show acceptance of a person when one sees who the person is. For example, usually when we recognize wealthy people or important officials, don't we tend to welcome them and give them preferential treatment? The Greek word refers to acts of partiality, respect of persons, snobbery, or personal favoritism.

Read Genesis 43:1-5 and 2 Samuel 14:23-24 for two examples of "receiving someone's face" as an example of favoritism.

The wording actually forbids a practice already in progress. As verses 5-9 suggest, James's readers already were giving special treatment to some wealthy people. Such favoritism had to stop. Those who believe in Jesus Christ should no longer make distinctions based on externals such as position, wealth, or power. If showing favoritism is wrong, doesn't that imply we should not seek or expect favoritism from others? Can we admit that we enjoy being on the receiving end of favoritism?

The pastor of a large, prominent church told this story on himself: One evening he stopped by the church to encourage choir members rehearsing for a musical presentation. Not intending to stay long, he parked in a no-parking area near the entrance. After a few minutes he left and drove home.

The next morning he found a note in his office mailbox. It read: "A small thing, but Tuesday night when you came to rehearsal, you parked in the 'No Parking' area. A reaction from one of my crew (who did not recognize you until after you got out of the car) was, 'There's another jerk parking in the "No Parking" area!' We try hard not to allow people—even workers—to park anywhere other than the parking lots. I would appreciate your cooperation too." A member of the maintenance staff had signed the note. The pastor's esteem for this staff member went up because he had the courage to call his pastor to accountability.

As the pastor had driven up that night, he admitted he had thought, *I shouldn't park here, but after all, I am the pastor.* That translates: *I'm an exception to the rules.* The pastor acknowledged he is not the exception to church rules or to God's rules. As a leader, he's to be an example, not an exception. Both showing and expecting favoritism are wrong.

Using a hypothetical case that apparently was hitting close to home, James described in verses 2-4 how Christians sometimes show favoritism. Two visitors, probably neither of whom were Christians, came into the "meeting." "Meeting" translates the Greek word usually rendered "synagogue." The term can mean "the place of meeting or the assembly of people." James, like other early Jewish believers, used this word to describe Christian worship for many years after Jesus' ascension.

The picture of two men entering the Christian assembly contrasted greatly. The first man was "wearing a gold ring, dressed in fine clothes," indicating wealth and importance. In the ancient world people wore many rings to show their wealth. "Fine" means "bright, shining, or radiant." As we might say, *He was dressed to the nines.* In sharp contrast the "poor man dressed in dirty clothes." The word for "poor" signifies "poverty-stricken, dependent on others for support." His shabby appearance indicated he probably was a beggar.

Those in a Christian gathering should have welcomed both visitors with equal warmth and consideration. James, however, described actions of favoritism the Lord condemns. The rich man was given special attention. Not only was he asked to sit but also was shown to a "good place."

In contrast, the poor man received no warm welcome. Instead, he was ordered to "stand over there," possibly in some remote corner at the back of the room. His other option was to sit "on the floor by my footstool." Deference was given to the rich man simply because of his outward appearance. The poor man received social snobbery and discrimination from these believers.

Using the past tense in verse 4, James asked a question that forced his readers to face the shame of what they, or some of them, already had done. At the least they had discriminated" among themselves. They had shown partiality to the rich.

In some contexts the word for "discriminated" can mean to waver, to doubt, to be at odds with." Perhaps it has that meaning here as it does in 1:6 ("doubting"). In discriminating between the rich and the poor, these believers had shown they doubted a basic tenet of their faith, namely that God loves and thus values every person, and He sent Jesus to die for everyone's sins so every person, without exception, would have the opportunity to believe and be saved.

The term also could indicate their actions were creating a division within their church, some contending for the rich and others for the poor. Whatever James's intended meaning, favoritism inevitably causes discord.

Because these Christians showed a preference for rich people over poor people, they were "judges with evil thoughts" (2:4). They become like judges who made judicial decisions without regard for what the evidence and justice dictated. They were making judgments about people's value on the basis of what those people had, not on the basis of who they were.

The believers were thinking of what rich people could do for them, not of what the gospel could do for rich people. Of course rich and poor alike are to be welcomed as individuals for whom the Lord shed His precious blood.

"The LORD does not look at the things man looks at. Man looks at the outward appearance, but the LORD looks at the heart." 1 Samuel 16:7, NIV

Content Points

1. We are all members of God's family and highly valued by Him, regardless of our differences.
2. Followers of Jesus Christ should not make distinctions based on externals such as position, wealth, or power.
3. We should not expect to be treated any differently than anyone else.
4. When we show favoritism of one person over another, we make ourselves judges, setting one person over the other.

Discussion Questions

1. In what circumstances do we sometimes tell ourselves, "It's OK; I'm an exception to the rules"?
2. How do we "size others up" and treat one differently from another?
3. Describe a time when you witnessed a rich or influential person being treated differently from others.
4. Have you ever seen that happen in church? If so, tell about it.

"Do not judge, so that you won't be judged. For with the judgment you use, you will be judged, and with the measure you use, it will be measured to you." Matthew 7:1

Notes

Application Idea
Make two lists of people by name in your church.
On the first list, include the names of

- those who are leaders
- those who are respected
- those who are influential
- those with social status

On the second list, include the names of

- those who are poor (and are obvious by the way they dress)
- those who are poorly educated
- those who are eccentric or "weird"
- the physically or mentally handicapped
- those who are socially obnoxious

As you look at the people on your lists, think about the way you interact with them at church. Describe your common behavior. Do you go out of your way to talk with those on the first list and avoid those on the second? Does your behavior betray an attitude of prejudice? At church, how do you need to adjust your thinking and your actions?

5*Listen, my dear brothers: Didn't God choose the poor in this world*
to be rich in faith and heirs of the kingdom that He has promised
to those who love Him? 6*Yet you dishonored that poor man. Don't*
the rich oppress you and drag you into the courts? 7*Don't they*
blaspheme the noble name that you bear? 8*If you really carry*
out the royal law prescribed in Scripture, Love your neighbor
as yourself, you are doing well. 9*But if you show favoritism, you*
commit sin and are convicted by the law as transgressors. 10*For*
whoever keeps the entire law, yet fails in one point, is guilty of
breaking it all. 11*For He who said, Do not commit adultery, also*
said, Do not murder. So if you do not commit adultery, but you do
murder, you are a lawbreaker.

II. *The Problems with Favoritism* (vv. 5-11)

If there were but one place in the world where discrimination should not exist, it would be the church. Discrimination is widely practiced everywhere. Church folk are to reach out to and welcome every person, regardless of outward appearances or circumstances. This Scripture shows three things wrong with favoritism.

[5]Listen, my dear brothers: Didn't God choose the poor in this world to be rich in faith and heirs of the kingdom that He has promised to those who love Him? [6]Yet you dishonored that poor man. Don't the rich oppress you and drag you into the courts? [7]Don't they blaspheme the noble name that you bear?

"But many who are first will be last, and the last first." Matthew 19:30

A. Favoritism Is Unreasonable (vv. 5-7)—Generally speaking, wealthy people are all for the status quo. Political or social change might threaten their wealth and position. Jesus demonstrated God's love for rich people and poor people, for religious people and secular people, for socially accepted people and social outcasts. He taught that the first would be last in the kingdom. He spoke of the blessings belonging to the poor. No wonder the rich persecuted Christians in New Testament times, judging and insulting them, and blaspheming the name of Jesus.

In essence James was saying, "Why are you worried about impressing such people? They're certainly not worried about impressing you. They're doing the opposite." God wants us to know that favoritism is unreasonable.

"Listen" was an orator-like call for attention, perhaps softened by "my dear brothers" (v. 5). James asked, "Didn't God choose the poor in this world to be rich in faith and heirs of the kingdom that He has promised to those who love Him?" The question anticipates an affirmative answer.

That God has chosen "the poor in this world" seems obvious (see **Going Deeper,** p. 64). Most early church members were poor, and some were even slaves. "In this world" probably means in the estimation "of the world." Even the poorest believers, however, were really rich from an eternal viewpoint. They were "heirs of the kingdom" of God. This kingdom will be inherited by all "those who love Him."

The bias of the believers toward poor visitors was wrong because it didn't parallel God's attitude toward them. Poor people are not the only ones who would be saved, of course. Not all of them would choose to receive salvation.

"Yet you dishonored that poor man." "You" is emphatic and contrasts their discrimination against the poor to God's glad acceptance of them. These Christians had treated the poor person like an unwanted tramp.

Content Points

1. In New Testament times, most Christians were poor and many were slaves.
2. In Christ, even the poorest person is rich in eternal things.
3. We dishonor the poor when we treat others better than them.

Notes

Discussion Questions

1. When a poor person comes into your church as a first-time visitor, how is he or she most likely to be treated?
2. What reasons—other than wealth—might lead those in the church not to treat a visitor well?
3. Is there any circumstance in which we can justify treating a person poorly?

Application Ideas

1. In the Sermon on the Mount (Matt. 5:21-30), Jesus "raised the bar" on our behavior. No longer was it enough to avoid actions, but our hearts must be pure so that our minds would not even think about sinful things. Read these verses to determine Jesus's teachings.
2. Think about the kinds of people about whom you harbor prejudice, misgivings, or mistrust. Jesus would challenge us not only to treat them better, but to stop thinking inappropriately about them. Is that a challenge for you?
3. Think of a specific individual that you need to change your attitude about. With God's help, will you do it?
4. What group or type of people do you need to change your attitude about? Again, with God's help, will you do it? If so, what actions will show your new heart?

B. Favoritism Is Misdirected (vv. 6-7)—James showed how horribly misdirected is favoritism shown to the wealthy. He asked, "Don't the rich oppress you?" His readers knew the rich as a class were indeed guilty of oppressing the poor, and especially the Christian poor. This mistreatment usually had to do with the personal debts of the poor.

Summary arrest, a legal empowerment that permitted a creditor to seize and drag a debtor right off the street and into court, was allowed in that day. The verb for "drag" sometimes has a gentle meaning, as in John 6:44, but here as in Acts 16:19 it signifies cruelty and violence. The believers' favoritism insulted impoverished fellow believers and honored spoiled and selfish oppressors.

Another reason these Christians' treatment of the rich was shameful stemmed from yet another rhetorical question demanding a yes answer. James asked, "Don't they blaspheme the noble name that you bear?" (v. 7). Of course they did. The Book of Acts records instances of just that. (See Acts 4:8-21; 5:12-40.) No law then forbade the worship of Christ, but the rich and influential needed none. Their wealth and power enabled them to harass Christians seemingly at will.

In their harassment of Christians (who mostly were poor), rich people blasphemed "the noble name" of Jesus. According to ancient tradition, the name of an owner was called aloud over a possession, such as land or a slave. This announced ownership and declared that the owner was responsible for the possession's well-being.

Just so, the name of Jesus was called over believers at their baptisms (Acts 2:38; 8:16; 10:47-48). Their being baptized in Jesus' name signified that they belonged to Him. Rich people who oppressed poor Christians were blaspheming the fair and sacred name of Jesus (see Acts 9:4).

These verses show that the gospel is especially valuable to the poor, for it welcomes those who typically are not welcomed. Those who feel worthless in the eyes of the world discover they are valuable in the eyes of God.

Content Points

1. In New Testament times, it was commonly the rich and powerful who were persecuting the Christians.
2. These Christian poor were often forcibly dragged into court by the rich for their inability to pay their debts.
3. The rich not only persecuted the poor, but blasphemed (mocked) the name of Christ.

Discussion Questions

1. How do we who "have" treat those who "have not"?
2. When someone owes us and does not satisfy the debt promptly, what should we do?

Application Idea

Think of someone you know in need—not just material need—but the need for friendship, an ear to listen, help with a project, or an affirming word. What will you do to help that person this week?

"Give to the one who asks you, and don't turn away from the one who wants to borrow from you."
Matthew 5:42

[8]If you really carry out the royal law prescribed in Scripture, Love your neighbor as yourself, you are doing well.

C. Favoritism Is Unloving (v. 8)—The command "love your neighbor as yourself" (Jas. 2:8) reminds us that we can't get away from the fact that we need each other. Part of loving one another is acknowledging and being grateful for our interdependence. Thus favoritism shows lack of love.

A few years ago a heavy ice storm hit part of the country. Many trees suffered significant damage. Interestingly the trees with the worst damage were those that stood all alone. Where trees stood in groves, the branches and even the trunks of trees were leaning against each other. That support often kept them from snapping off. When we play favorites, we are deliberately cutting off some people from the support they need and depriving ourselves of the support they might offer us.

In verse 8 James may have answered an objection he expected from some of his readers. They could have asked,

Notes

"Love your neighbor as yourself."
Leviticus 19:18b

"The commandments:
Do not commit adultery,
Do not murder,
Do not steal,
Do not covet,
and if there is any other commandment—all are summed up by this: Love your neighbor as yourself."
Romans 13:9-10

"Aren't we supposed to love wealthy people too?" More likely he was making sure that what he had written in verses 5-7 would not be misunderstood. After all, he did not want to fan the fires of prejudice toward either the rich or the poor.

Some believers may have justified their favoritism toward the rich by saying they simply were showing love to them. So James was telling them that if they "really carry out the royal law", fine; they were "doing well" (v. 8). Their treatment of the poor called in question their motives.

The term "royal law" probably refers to the second half of Leviticus 19:18. Several reasons have been suggested for calling this "the royal law"—It was the king of laws, the law of the kingdom, fit to guide kings, the supreme law, or the law approved by the King (Matt. 22:39). The Law and the Prophets depended on this commandment as its cornerstone (v. 40).

All of these interpretations offer good suggestions. Whatever the meaning of the title, the command to love our neighbors is without doubt the undergirding principle of Christian conduct (Rom. 13:9-10). Christian love has no room for favoritism.

Content Point

The "royal law" capsulates everything we need to know and do in our relationships with other people.

Discussion Questions

1. Why is it so hard to love others as we love ourselves?
2. What are we supposed to do when others aren't easy to love?

Application Idea

Do your actions toward all people demonstrate the "royal law" of loving others as you love yourself? Consider how you could treat others better. How can you start to do that this week?

9But if you show favoritism, you commit sin and are convicted by the law as transgressors. 10For whoever keeps the entire law, yet fails in one point, is guilty of breaking it all. 11For He who said, Do not commit adultery, also said, Do not murder. So if you do not commit adultery, but you do murder, you are a lawbreaker.

D. Favoritism Is Unchristian (vv. 9-11)—Whether we admit it or not, most of us struggle against certain prejudices that affect our reactions and responses to people. These prejudices could be against divorced people, the emotionally ill, or those who differ with us on philosophy, politics, language, or religion. Such prejudice operating within a church produces cliques, gossip, legalism, and power groups.

To show favoritism is to act in an unchristian manner toward others.

The Christians James addressed were showing favoritism against the poor who came into their meetings. In responding lovingly toward the rich, they had depreciated the poor; but the royal law demands equal treatment of both groups. It forbids any partiality in the church.

Showing favoritism is no simple breach of etiquette. To practice partiality is to "commit sin" (Jas. 2:9), literally, "to work sin." Those guilty of this sin were already "convicted" of violating the royal law of Leviticus 19:18. This offense was a serious matter for good reason. A cliquish church cannot reach the masses.

Both verses 10 and 11 begin with "for," which in each case introduces proof that favoritism is morally a violation of God's law. Even if a believer keeps "the entire law," but "fails in one point," that believer is "guilty of breaking it all" (v. 10). The principle is clear: One who violates one of God's laws is guilty of violating all of them.

"By this all people will know that you are My disciples, if you have love for one another." John 13:35

Two things in verse 10 might bother us. **First** is the idea of living a lifetime and keeping all but one law. No one could ever come close to doing that. However, James was not being hopelessly idealistic but rather was making a point in a dramatic fashion. No one could miss it. We only have to commit one sin to be placed in the camp of sinners.

Second, the idea of being guilty of the entire law if we violate only one law does not sound fair to us. We could argue with this Scripture, but we will do better to learn from it. God's law is portrayed as a whole. To break any part of it is to break the whole law. Think of children playing baseball and one of them hits the ball through a nearby window with six panes. The child broke only one pane; five were still intact. Nevertheless, the window as a whole is broken; it no longer provides an effective barrier against wind and rain.

One transgression shatters the principle of obedience. The authority of God is ultimate. He wants His children to obey all of His will, not just part of it. To break the perfect unity of His expressed will is to fracture it in its entirety. This understanding magnifies for us that the salvation we receive by faith depends totally on the righteousness of Jesus Himself. By pondering verse 10, we can more fully appreciate the enormity of our sin and the encompassing scope of God's grace.

Notes

Content Points

1. Prejudice at work within a church produces cliques, gossip, legalism, and power groups.
2. Showing favoritism is to "commit sin."
3. The sin of favoritism is just as serious a sin as any other sin (v. 10) and cannot be excused.
4. God's law is a whole. To break one point is the same as breaking it all. It is all rebellion against God.

Discussion Questions

1. We sometimes (often) put sins into different categories: "big" sins and "little" sins. What did James say about that viewpoint?
2. Look at verse 10: "For whoever keeps the entire law, yet fails in one point, is guilty of breaking it all." How does this principle destroy the concept of "big sins" and "little sins"?

Application Ideas

1. In your quiet time alone with God, list the "little sins" in your life. How "little" do you think they are to God?
2. After confessing your sins (1 John 1:9), pray for the Holy Spirit to help you overcome them.
3. Now choose one "little sin" from your list and pray for wisdom (Jas. 1:5) to know how to take action to defeat it.

12Speak and act as those who will be judged by the law of freedom. 13For judgment is without mercy to the one who hasn't shown mercy. Mercy triumphs over judgment.

III. *The Prescription for Avoiding Favoritism* (vv. 12-13)

If favoritism is so wrong, how can we avoid it? Verses 12-13 give a two-part prescription to help us. If we keep both parts filled and up-to-date, we can avoid favoritism.

12Speak and act as those who will be judged by the law of freedom.

A. Live in Light of Judgment (v. 12)—James ended his discussion on showing favoritism with an exhortation and warning (2:12-13). He appealed to his readers to obey the royal law in both their speech and actions. The present tense of the commands "speak and act" indicates continuing action (v. 12). God wants us to know we are accountable to Him for consistently showing love in what we say as well as in what we do. Love ensures that we will treat all people right.

Unloving behavior, such as discrimination against others based on their economic status or anything else, "will be judged" (v. 12). Let us speak and act with the awareness that we too will face judgment. God will judge us all.

The standard of judgment for believers will be "the law of freedom" (v. 12). This is not a freedom to disobey God's commands. The Mosaic law was a law of bondage. Sinful humans failed to keep it and were bound in its penalties.

Christ frees those who place their faith in Him. He delivers them from the penalty and the power of sin. The indwelling Holy Spirit empowers believers, thus freeing them to obey God (Rom. 8:1-4).

Christians are to live under the liberating law of freedom, which in this context can be understood as the royal law of love on which God's entire moral law is based. We will be judged on how well we practice love toward all other people, regardless of who they are or what they are like.

What was God saying in James about our churches today? The church that accepts, appreciates, and affirms all people is the church that God blesses. Right behavior won't happen accidentally. It requires a deliberate effort by each member. Everybody contributes to the atmosphere of the church either negatively or positively. Would people come back to your church because of your warmth and acceptance?

If we can't learn to welcome one another here on the earth, what makes us think we'll get along together in heaven? With some people we may have to use a little creativity to get along. Maybe we just need to learn how to value difficult people for their uniqueness. Remembering that we'll be judged helps us accept others—and that helps us avoid favoritism.

Content Points

1. Christians are to live under the liberating law of freedom, which is the royal law of love (Lev. 19:18; Matt. 22:39) on which the entire moral law of God is based.
2. We will be judged on how well we practice love toward all people, regardless of who they are or what they are like. How else will we get along in heaven?
3. The indwelling Holy Spirit empowers believers, thus freeing them to obey God (Rom. 8:1-4).
4. The church that accepts, appreciates, and affirms all people is the church that God blesses.

Discussion Questions

1. When a person of color, a poor person, or someone who obviously doesn't "fit" socially comes into your church, how do you think that person is made to feel?

Notes

"Blessed are the merciful, because they will be shown mercy." Matthew 5:7

"Be merciful, just as your Father also is merciful." Luke 6:36

2. Do you quickly and naturally speak to them and welcome them? Do you do more than give them a quick smile and handshake and then walk away?
3. In what ways do you think your church might be blessed if it were more accepting of others?

Application Ideas

1. If you were judged today for how you have been treating others, what judgment would you receive?
2. List attitudes and behaviors you would need to change to escape God's judgment in this matter.
2. Put yourself in the place of an "outsider" who visits your church. What actions might help you feel accepted?

[13]For judgment is without mercy to the one who hasn't shown mercy. Mercy triumphs over judgment.

B. Show Mercy (v. 13)—Individuals who show no mercy will receive no mercy at the time of judgment. "Mercy" is a feeling of compassion that is expressed in action. Believers have received mercy from God. Therefore they should act mercifully toward others.

James was not teaching salvation by works (showing mercy). He was saying that merciful attitudes and actions give proof that individuals are indeed Christians. As children of God, believers should reflect His character of love, compassion, and merciful behavior.

Finally, James affirmed positively that "mercy triumphs over judgment" (2:13). This clause can be translated in several glad ways: Mercy rejoices over, exults over, glories over, and even overcomes judgment. This general principle springs from the gospel itself. God's saving grace and forgiveness of sins result in mercy for condemned sinners. The cross of Christ means Christians have no fear of eternal condemnation in judgment. Mercy triumphs.

A beautiful example of practicing the royal law of love occurred years ago during a worship service in a church across the street from a college campus. The church members customarily wore their finest to church, so everyone was well-dressed. One Sunday Bill decided to attend. He had wild hair. He wore a T-shirt with holes in it, jeans, and no shoes.

This was his typical wardrobe for his entire four years of college. He was kind of different but brilliant, and he became a Christian while attending college. He walked into the service wearing his usual wardrobe. The service already had begun as Bill started down the aisle looking for a seat. The auditorium was completely packed, so he just sat down on the carpet near the front.

By now the tension in the air was thick. From the back of the church, a deacon slowly began making his way toward Bill. A dignified, godly man, this deacon was in his 80s. He had silver-gray hair and wore a three-piece suit. As he started toward the student, everyone was thinking, *You can't blame him for asking the kid to leave. How could you expect a man of his age and background to understand some college kid who dresses like that and sits on the floor?*

The minister couldn't even preach his sermon because all the people were watching the two. As the deacon reached Bill, he dropped his cane on the floor. With great difficulty he lowered himself and sat down next to the student. When the minister gained control, he said, "What I'm about to preach, you will never remember. What you have just seen, you will never forget."

A lack of mercy in any life suggests a person has not genuinely repented and received God's mercy in Christ. Showing mercy helps us avoid playing favorites. We relate to others according to God's Word when we express love to them by showing mercy.

Content Points

1. God's saving grace and forgiveness of sins result in mercy for condemned sinners.
2. Merciful attitudes and actions give proof that individuals are indeed Christians.
3. We avoid playing favorites when we express love by showing mercy.

Discussion Question

Think about the definition given for *mercy—a feeling of compassion that is expressed in action.* Now consider Romans 5:8—"God proves His own love for us in that while we were still sinners Christ died for us!" As God "proved" His love for us at the cross, what are some ways we can "prove" we are merciful to others?

Appllication Idea

Think about the people in your life: family, neighbors, co-workers, church members. List some tangible ways you show mercy to those who need it.

1.

2.

3.

4.

Notes

"This is what the L*ORD says:*
The wise must not boast in his wisdom; the mighty must not boast in his might; the rich must not boast in his riches. But the one who boasts should boast in this, that he understands and knows Me—that I am the L*ORD, showing faithful love, justice, and righteousness on the earth, for I delight in these things."* Jeremiah 9:23-24

SUMMARY

1. Favoritism refers to acts of partiality, disrespect of persons, snobbery, or personal favor of one over another. James used the example of a rich man and poor man who both visited a worship service. The rich man received preferential seating and treatment.

2. Favoritism is unreasonable, misdirected, unloving, and unchristian.

3. The "royal law" (2.8) probably refers to Leviticus 19:18 which encapsulates everything we need to know and do in our relationships with other people.

4. The "law of freedom" is a reference to the "royal law" to love, which is the foundation of all of God's moral law.

5. Favoritism can be avoided as we show mercy to others as God has shown mercy to us.

5Listen, my dear brothers: Didn't God choose the poor in this world to be rich in faith and heirs of the kingdom that He has promised to those who love Him?

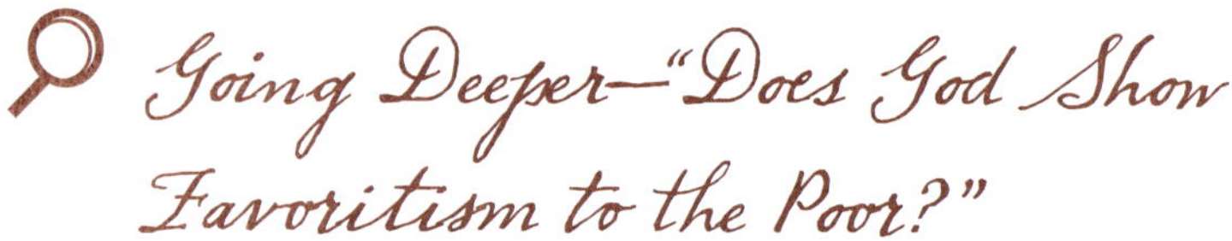

In this passage against showing favoritism, do the words "Didn't God choose the poor?" mean He shows favoritism to poor people? The answer is no. His words simply reflect the poor economic status of the majority of believers. To infer that God plays favorites would be a mistake for three reasons.

First, *other Scriptures make clear that "God doesn't show favoritism, but in every nation the person who fears Him and does righteousness is acceptable to Him" (Acts 10:34-35). John 3:16 describes His sacrificial love for "the world," and that means everyone alike. Revelation 3:17-20 invites all people everywhere, rich and poor, to receive the gift of salvation. Also, the New Testament mentions rich believers, among them Joseph of Arimathea and Philemon.*

Second, *the majority of believers in New Testament times were relatively poor. For example, 1 Corinthians 1:26-31 describes the believers in the Corinthian church. Among them were a few considered to be wise, powerful, or of noble birth. But from the world's perspective, the other believers were viewed as foolish, weak, insignificant, and despised. On* *the whole, they were from the lower economic strata of society. (Anywhere in the world, people considered to be wealthy are a minority. Thus their numbers in the overall Christian community always will be relatively small.)*

Third, *wealthy people are prone to trust their wealth rather than God. Not all of them do that, but many do. Colossians 3:5 describes greed as idolatry. Matthew 19:16-26 tells of the rich man who asked Jesus how to enter the kingdom of heaven. Apparently because the man trusted more in his riches than in God, Jesus told him to give away all he had. He refused, and Jesus commented on how hard it would be for rich people to trust in God rather than their wealth. Jesus also said, "You cannot be slaves of God and of money" (Matt. 6:24).*

"It is easier for a camel to go through the eye of a needle than for a rich person to enter the kingdom of God."
Matthew 19:24

JAMES 2:14-26

[14]What good is it, my brothers, if someone says he has faith, but
does not have works? Can his faith save him? [15]If a brother or
sister is without clothes and lacks daily food, [16]and one of you
says to them, "Go in peace, keep warm, and eat well," but you
don't give them what the body needs, what good is it? [17]In the
same way faith, if it doesn't have works, is dead by itself.

[18]But someone will say, "You have faith, and I have works."
Show me your faith without works, and I will show you faith
from my works. [19]You believe that God is one; you do well. The
demons also believe—and they shudder.

[20]Foolish man! Are you willing to learn that faith without
works is useless? [21]Wasn't Abraham our father justified by works
when he offered Isaac his son on the altar? [22]You see that faith
was active together with his works, and by works, faith was
perfected. [23]So the Scripture was fulfilled that says, Abraham
believed God, and it was credited to him for righteousness, and
he was called God's friend. [24]You see that a man is justified by
works and not by faith alone. [25]And in the same way, wasn't
Rahab the prostitute also justified by works when she received
the messengers and sent them out by a different route? [26]For
just as the body without the spirit is dead, so also faith without
works is dead.

Lesson Four

DEMONSTRATE YOUR FAITH (JAMES 2:14-26)

I. **Faith and Inaction (2:14-17)**

II. **Faith and Action (2:18-20)**

III. **Faith in Action (2:21-26)**

A. Demonstrated by Obeying God (vv. 21-24)

B. Demonstrated by Assisting God's People (vv. 25-26)

LEARNING GOALS

As a result of studying this lesson, learners will:

- *See how Paul's and James's teachings about faith and works are complementary*
- *Evaluate the genuineness and depth of their own faith*
- *Describe ways faith is demonstrated by works*
- *Explain the relationship between faith and works*
- *Gain assurance of their salvation*

Notes

"Test yourselves [to see] if you are in the faith. Examine yourselves. Or do you not recognize for yourselves that Jesus Christ is in you?—unless you fail the test" 2 Corinthians 13:5.

We are saved by faith alone, but not by faith that is alone.

Children used to sing what their teachers called an action song. Each verse had this line, "If you're happy and you know it, then your face (hands, feet) will surely show it." A religious version of the song refers to showing you are saved by the way you live—"your life will surely show it." There is some pretty good theology in those words.

In fact, they are exactly what James declared in 2:14-26. Genuine faith produces good works. What art collector would rather have a bad copy than an original work of art? We're all interested in the real deal, the genuine article, the authentic original. As you study this Scripture, allow it to shed light on your claim to have placed your faith in the Lord Jesus Christ and your faithfulness to Him.

[14]What good is it, my brothers, if someone says he has faith, but
does not have works? Can his faith save him? [15]If a brother or sister
is without clothes and lacks daily food, [16]and one of you says to
them, "Go in peace, keep warm, and eat well," but you don't give
them what the body needs, what good is it? [17]In the same way faith,
if it doesn't have works, is dead by itself.

I. *Faith and Inaction* (vv. 14-17)

Before delving into these verses, let us acknowledge that some Bible scholars have debated whether the teachings about salvation from Paul and James conflict with each other. Paul taught we are saved by grace, not works; James said faith apart from works would not save anyone. As you study these verses, see if you do not agree that James wrote about works in terms of practical actions that demonstrate faith, while Paul wrote of works as acts that some incorrectly believed would earn acceptance with God. (See **Going Deeper,** p. 80.)

So what did James say? He began in 2:14, "What good is it, my brothers," James asked, "if someone says he has faith, but does not have works" (literally, "keeps on not having works"). It's a rhetorical question. The obvious answer is: *No good at all.* Another rhetorical question follows—"Can his faith save him?" Grammatically this question might be translated, "That kind of faith can't save such a person, can it?" Again, the obvious answer is no. Read 2 Corinthians 13:5.

We are saved by faith alone, but not by faith that is alone. Fruit accompanies genuine saving faith; faith is not found in the empty wastes of hollow words. If professed faith makes no difference in everyday living, it does not pass the test of real faith. Let us be clear about what faith is.

James and Paul spoke of faith in terms of trust expressed in a faith commitment to Jesus as Messiah, Savior, and Lord. Paul stressed that this faith alone brought salvation, and James declared that saving faith cannot lie dormant in believers' hearts, allowing them to live loveless, unconcerned lives.

Faith is more than religious talk or opinions. Real faith motivates believers to practical service rooted in love for God and people. To make that point, James continued, "If a brother or sister is without clothes and lacks daily food, and one of you says to them, 'Go in peace, keep warm, and eat well,' but you don't give them what the body needs, what good is it?" (2:15-16).

The needy person in this illustration was either "a brother or sister," which indicates he or she had some close relationship with the church. The words likely indicate church membership. "Is without clothes" does not indicate literal nakedness. It probably points to an ongoing lack of basic physical necessities, not just an emergency situation.

This illustration may even suggest the problem had existed when the person's relationship with the church was first established. The constancy of this problem meant the congregation could not easily overlook the situation.

"Lacks daily food," of course, indicates utter destitution. When Jesus said that the impoverished would always be with us (Matt. 26:11), He was not depreciating the unfortunate people of the world. He simply stated a fact. Poor fellow believers are an ongoing challenge to the faith of more fortunate Christians.

"One of you" could have been any of James's readers. All of them were aware of the widespread poverty in their midst. In the face of economic need in the Jerusalem area, Paul had effectively reminded churches he founded about their obligation to help the poor Christians there.

Those far-off churches had been so moved by Paul's appeal that collectively they took up an offering and sent it by the concerned apostle to the needy believers in Jerusalem. Paul had urged the offering probably to underscore the caring brother-sister relationship that should exist between fellow Christians of all cultures and levels. (See 2 Cor. 8:1-9; Rom. 15:25-27.)

Did James know about this generous collection when he wrote? Perhaps. Regardless, callous refusal to care for the physical needs of fellow Christians did call for attention—and correction. Perhaps James chose to use this illustration to make his point about how real faith manifests itself.

James may have pictured what he knew to be a common occurrence. Perhaps a church member had responded to a brother or sister's request for help with "Go in peace, be warm and eat well," but gave no practical help at all. "Go in peace" commonly was used as we use "goodbye" today. In the absence of help, the expression was a brush-off. The response meant simply, "I hope you get some help somehow, but don't count on me." It was a mockery if the one asked could have helped. The next question sums up this poignant point: "What good is it?" Indeed, of what benefit was that response

either to the poor or to the one who could have helped? It helped neither but seriously hurt both.

What about people who wander into a church or stand outside and beg for money as members leave? Appearances can be deceiving. In a small Texas church a young woman came into the sanctuary in a T-shirt, tattered jeans, and tennis shoes. Instead of sitting in a pew, she chose to sit in the ledge of one of the stained glass windows. She left as the service ended.

She came back the next Sunday and sat in the same place. Several church members asked the pastor what they needed to do to help this poor woman. One Sunday, the pastor literally caught hold of her arm as she was barreling out the door. She promised to meet with him at a certain date and time.

It turned out that she was from a wealthy family and was rejecting their passion for material things. The church kept extending love and concern for her until she had dealt with her issues to the extent that she went back to college.

Similar people come to a church long enough to get some bills paid by the members and then disappear. God's people must take precaution to recognize a genuine need. Why? Because helping such individuals perpetuates their problems. The church must be Spirit-led and wise in its care for others.

James was not encouraging enabling behavior or guilt trips if a person is turned away because he or she would only accept money—not gas, food, clothing, or other help.

James's illustration is clear and compelling. We can easily understand it because most of us have been there at one time or another. Warm, fuzzy, spiritual-sounding words won't get the job done when need is staring us in the face. An exhortation to keep a positive attitude during a time of personal crisis and need will not suffice. The proof of real faith in a situation like the one described in verses 15-16 is to provide real food and real clothes.

First John 3:17-18 says, "If anyone has the world's goods, and sees his brother in need but shuts off his compassion from him—how can God's love reside in him? Little children, we must not love in word or speech, but in deed and truth."

In verse 17 James drove home his point that faith is more than an intellectual acceptance of a truth. Faith surrenders to Christ's will and direction. "If [faith] doesn't have works" means literally "if faith should keep on not having works." James was not talking about a surprise audit of a single transaction. None of us can honestly claim we act on our faith 100 percent of the time. Believers are faulty human beings who can make the wrong choices and at times fail to follow our Lord.

James was not talking about believers' struggles in living the life of faith. He was talking about a lifestyle. A so-called faith that cannot be detected in the daily life and works of a so-called believer cannot be saving faith. That kind of faith is dead by itself." Innately, a workless faith is indeed useless to self-deluded believers as well as to hungry beggars. Faith that produces no works is dead.

Content Points

1. James wrote about works in terms of practical actions that demonstrate faith, while Paul wrote of works as acts that some incorrectly believed would earn acceptance with God.
2. We are saved by faith alone, but not by faith that is alone. By our fruit, we are known.
3 Faith motivates believers to practical service rooted in love for God and people.
4. Real faith causes us to be involved, not indifferent.
5. A so-called faith that cannot be detected in the daily life and works of a so-called believer cannot be saving faith. Although we are not to judge others, we can be fruit inspectors!

Discussion Questions

1. Look again at 2 Corinthians 13:5. What things should comprise the "test" of which Paul spoke?
2. Do you think most Christians give themselves this kind of test? Do they test themselves regularly?
3. Is our testing sincere, transparent, and a true desire to discover the answers?
4. Is our attitude expressed with a humble, contrite, and repentant spirit?

Application Ideas

1. As you think about the "test" of genuine faith in 2 Corinthians 13:5, when was the last time you gave yourself a good self-examination? This week spend time with God giving your faith a good check-up.
2. Ask yourself the questions the group discussed about our self-examinations:
    - Do you do it with sincerity, transparency, and a true desire to discover the answers? (Ps. 25:4-5; 119:10)
    - Do you do it with a humble, contrite spirit? (Ps. 51:17; 1 Pet. 5:5b-6)
    - Do you do it with a repentant attitude? (1 John 1:9; Ps. 66:18-19; 19:12-13)
3. Think about a situation when someone asked you for help and you didn't give it, even though you had the ability and/or resources to do so. What would make you act differently in the future?

"Make Your ways known to me, LORD; teach me Your paths. Guide me in Your truth and teach me, for You are the God of my salvation." Psalm 25:4-5

"God resists the proud, but gives grace to the humble. Humble yourselves therefore under the mighty hand of God, so that He may exalt you in due time." 1 Peter 5:5-6

Notes

4. Read the following passages. Based on each passage, what does your response to those in need indicate about your faith relationship with Christ?

Matthew 25:31-46	1 John 3:17-18
Acts 2:45	Galatians 6:9-10
Hebrews 13:16	Ephesians 2:10

18But someone will say, "You have faith, and I have works." Show me
your faith without works, and I will show you faith from my works.
19You believe that God is one; you do well. The demons also believe—
and they shudder. 20Foolish man! Are you willing to learn that faith
without works is useless?

II. Faith and Action (vv. 18-20)

The lack of punctuation marks in the Greek manuscripts preserving New Testament texts complicates efforts to interpret James 2:18. We do not know for certain the identity of the "someone" James imagined to break into his argument. Was he a friend or an opponent to James's teaching or was this James himself? How much of this verse did the "someone" say, and to whom did the "you" and the "I" refer? While the details of interpretation in this brief passage may differ according to the decision made about these matters, the overall message remains clear.

This study assumes James to be the "someone." He addressed his readers as though they were a single person, saying in effect, *You claim to have faith, and I know I have works.* An undemonstrated faith could only be an intellectual acceptance of a teaching, not a commitment to a living Lord. As though they were present, James challenged his readers: "Show me your faith without works." Appropriately, the words translated "show me" mean "to bring to light, to display or exhibit." In this context the sense is "give proof to me." Of course, proving "faith without works" presents a challenge that cannot be met.

However, James went on to say with confidence, "I will show (prove to) you faith from (out of) my works." Works do not achieve salvation, but they result from salvation. James refused to allow us to back into some corner and pronounce theological affirmations about our faith in God without validating those affirmations by our works and deeds of service in the kingdom.

Faith that is merely the acceptance of a creed does not produce works of love and helpfulness. Therefore in verse 19 James commented on fruitless orthodoxy. He said, "You believe that God is one," summarizing Deuteronomy 6:4. The Jewish name for the confession in Deuteronomy 6:4 is "Shema" and means "hear."

In that day devout Jews were careful to repeat the Shema at least twice daily. They believed this practice protected them from evil and even cooled the fires of Gehenna. They believed this recitation had saving power and were sure the very parchment on which this verse was written prevented the approach of demons.

The statement of belief "that God is one" can mean either that there is just one God (monotheism) or that God in His personality is one. Both meanings are true, and both state an important doctrine. So James said to those orthodox believers, "You do well." He might have added, *but not well enough.* Simply believing either in the existence or the oneness of God is not saving faith.

To drive this point home James added, "The demons also believe—and they shudder." Even the demons have an orthodox belief, but they're still demons facing God's ultimate condemnation and judgment. At least those evil spirits shuddered. Many of these readers had made no practical response to their orthodoxy at all. The point is clear—just believing something about God is not saving faith. Merely knowing biblical truth about God provides no eternal security.

Merely knowing biblical truth about God provides no eternal security.

In verse 20, still speaking to the objector or to his readers as though they were a single objector to his argument, James continued—"Foolish man!" "Foolish" carries the idea of being "empty headed," stressing the dullness of the objector. "Are you willing to learn that faith without works is useless?" The tense of "to learn" makes it mean "to know once and for all."

The wording of the question suggests James suspected his readers were unwilling to learn. If the imagined objector was willing to look at biblical proof, James was ready and able to provide it. "Useless" conveys the idea of barrenness. It describes "faith without works" as being nonproductive, like uninvested money or unplanted land.

In verses 18-20, James was not demeaning an intelligent faith, but rather he was warning against a superficial and useless claim to faith. As we reflect on these verses, let us take time to list differences our faith has made in our lives. Are we growing in our faith, allowing the Lord to lead us into untried paths of service? Do our checkbooks reflect a true trust and commitment to God and His kingdom's priorities? Are our relationships and contacts with others kind, thoughtful, and helpful? Let's renew our commitment to living out our faith in our living Lord.

Renew your commitment to living out your faith in the living Lord.

CONTENT POINTS

1. Simply believing either in the existence or the oneness of God is not saving faith.
2. Our works are "proof" of our faith.
3. Believing that God exists or even believing correct doctrine about God is not the same as saving faith.

Notes

Discussion Questions

1. Do we ever substitute right doctrine for right action? What else do we substitute as proof of our faith?
2. If James were a "country boy" today, he might say, "The proof is in the eating of the pudding." In the "pudding" of our daily lives, what would demonstrate or prove our faith?

Application Ideas

1. Name three things you have done this week that would demonstrate your faith to a casual observer.
2. What are some things you aren't doing but should and can do to demonstrate your faith?
3. What practical differences does your faith make in:
   - how you spend your time
   - how you spend your money
   - how you manage relationships
   - how temperament and personality
   - how you serve God and others

[21]Wasn't Abraham our father justified by works when he offered
Isaac his son on the altar? [22]You see that faith was active together
with his works, and by works, faith was perfected. [23]So the Scripture
was fulfilled that says, Abraham believed God, and it was credited
to him for righteousness, and he was called God's friend. [24]You see
that a man is justified by works and not by faith alone. [25]And in the
same way, wasn't Rahab the prostitute also justified by works when
she received the messengers and sent them out by a different route?
[26]For just as the body without the spirit is dead, so also faith with-
out works is dead.

III. *Faith in Action* (vv. 21-26)

Retired senior pastor John Bisagno of Houston's First Baptist Church offered a compelling illustration of faith in his book, *The Power of Positive Praying.* One afternoon John was absorbed in reading a book when his young daughter came to him and asked for a doll house."

Absentmindedly, her father said he would and went back to reading the book. Then John heard the back door of the house opening and shutting several times. He looked out the window of his study. His daughter was carrying all of her dolls, toys, and dishes to a corner of the backyard.

He asked his wife to explain what she was doing.

His wife replied, "Oh, you promised her a doll house and she believes you. She's just getting ready for it."[1]

Melodye Jan had faith in action. By faith she believed her father would build her a doll house, and she acted on that faith. This story may also teach us to watch what we promise!

As examples of faith in action, James called attention to two Old Testament personalities, Abraham and Rahab. Why these two people? Perhaps he chose them in order to highlight two different actions that validate faith.

[21]Wasn't Abraham our father justified by works when he offered Isaac his son on the altar? [22]You see that faith was active together with his works, and by works, faith was perfected. [23]So the Scripture was fulfilled that says, Abraham believed God, and it was credited to him for righteousness, and he was called God's friend.

A. Demonstrated by Obeying God (vv. 21-24)—Identifying "Abraham" as "our Father" (Jas. 2:21) did not necessarily mean the readers were all Jewish Christians. The New Testament teaches that all believers, whether Jew or Gentile, become spiritual children of Abraham when they trust Christ to be their Savior (Rom. 4:1,11; Gal. 3:7).

James introduced the first action that proved faith with a rhetorical question: "Wasn't Abraham our father justified by works when he offered Isaac his son on the altar?" (Jas. 2:21; see Gen. 22:1-19). If this verse is taken out of context, it seems to teach we earn our justification (being declared just in God's sight). Taken in context it teaches justification is a gift of God received by faith, and obedience to God demonstrates that faith.

Let's review the background. Genesis 15:1-6 recounts Abraham's lament to the Lord that he had no heir. The Lord responded by promising him a son whose descendants would be as numerous as the visible stars. Genesis 15:6 says "Abram believed the Lord, and He credited it to him as righteousness."

Thirty years later the Lord commanded Abraham to offer as a sacrifice the son God had given him. Of course, the Lord did not actually allow Abraham to slay his son, but Abraham's willingness to do so was grounded in his faith that God would be true to His promise given 30 years before. James 2:21-24 uses Abraham's experience to illustrate three closely related points.

First, "faith was active together with his works" (v. 22). This stresses that faith is not some passive acceptance of religious truth. Biblical faith is a living reality that has to express itself in action. In Abraham's case, his faith was active with works that showed his faith to be real. The tense of "was active" indicates this cooperation also had been going on; it was nothing new.

Second, by Abraham's obedience in preparing to sacrifice Isaac, his "faith was perfected." "Perfected" means it was carried to its expected end; it was complete. James was not questioning Abraham's faith in the years before this experience with Isaac. Abraham had displayed his faith earlier in costly acts of obedience. However, Genesis 15:6 (quoted in

"Abram believed the Lord, and He credited it to him as righteousness."
Genesis 15:6

"By faith Abraham, when he was tested, offered up Isaac; he who had received the promises was offering up his only son, about whom it had been said, In Isaac your seed will be called. He considered God to be able even to raise someone from the dead, from which he also got him back as an illustration."
Hebrews 11:17-19

Notes

"Abraham believed God, and it was credited to him for righteousness." Romans 4:3

"Just as Abraham believed God, and it was credited to him for righteousness." Galatians 3:6

"Are You not our God who drove out the inhabitants of this land before Your people Israel and who gave it forever to the descendants of Abraham Your friend?" 2 Chronicles 20:7

Jas. 2:23) refers to Abraham's faith in the promise that God would produce through Abraham's son countless descendents. Did Abraham believe God would do that even if his son were dead? Evidently (see Heb. 11:17-19).

Abraham was sure that the Lord is not only all-powerful but also all-wise, all-good, and all-loving. Abraham demonstrated his faith by being willing to offer up his only son. His faith "was perfected" in that this supreme act of obedience grew from it and fully authenticated it.

Third, this act "fulfilled" Genesis 15:6 (Jas. 2:23). Abraham's obedient act of offering Isaac validated the Lord's gift of righteousness to Abraham on the basis of Abraham's faith. Thus to say this scriptural record was "fulfilled" is accurate. Abraham demonstrated he had indeed been justified long before he had believed.

Paul also quoted Genesis 15:6 (Rom. 4:3 and Gal. 3:6) but with a different purpose than that of James. Paul used it to show that Abraham was declared righteous before his circumcision, thus denying justification came through any ritual or any other work. James, of course, used that verse to show that Abraham's faith proved to be genuine when it was accompanied by works.

The Old Testament called Abraham "God's friend" (2 Chron. 20:7), perhaps because God saw fit to let him in on divine deliberations (Gen. 18:17). This complimentary term was used often by Jews when referring to Abraham. Perhaps James meant to suggest we believers customarily should be in friendly communication with God to learn from Him our moral and ethical duties.

James drew the obvious conclusion to this illustration about Abraham in verse 24. "You" in this verse is plural, which indicates James again was addressing all the people and not just the fanciful "foolish man" of verse 20. This dull imaginary opponent may have missed the main point, but James wanted his readers to grasp it. He saw that the life of justification begins with faith, but he saw also that this life is a life of obedience, love, and service.

The form of the Greek verb translated "justified" can mean "is shown to be justified." The matter and the measure of one's faith are always invisible to others. The presence and depth of that faith can be proved only by the believer's outward actions; that is James's point. To be sure, justification does come by faith; but that faith, like Abraham's, responds to God's commands with obedience. So James taught justification is by faith alone, but not by a faith that is alone.

Contents Points

1. Faith is not a passive acceptance of religious truth. Biblical faith is a living reality expressed in action.
2. Abraham's obedience in offering Isaac authenticated his faith as mature and complete.
3. Abraham's obedience in Genesis 22:1-18 validated God's gift of righteousness in Genesis 15:6.
4. Abraham's faith relationship with God earned him the distinction of being called "God's friend."

Discussion Questions

1. If Abraham had refused God's instruction to sacrifice Isaac, what would that say about his faith?
2. Verse 22 (NIV) says that Abraham's faith and his actions were working together and his faith was made complete by what he did. How did Abraham's actions make his faith complete?
3. What are the implications of being called "God's friend"? Is that a description to which we can realistically aspire?

Application Ideas

1. *The Message* renders 2:23 this way: "It's that mesh of believing and acting that got Abraham named 'God's friend.'" Think about how your lifestyle and actions go with what you profess to believe. Do they "mesh"?
2. Based on your believing and acting, would God call you His "friend"? If not, what would need to change in your life to make it so?
3. James describes the combination of action with Abraham's faith as making his faith *perfect* (HCSB, KJV, NASB) or *complete* (NIV, NLT). What do you believe this adjective "complete" means?
4. Can you describe yourself as complete? What one thing can you do this week to continue the "perfecting" process?

[25]And in the same way, wasn't Rahab the prostitute also justified by works when she received the messengers and sent them out by a different route? [26]For just as the body without the spirit is dead, so also faith without works is dead.

B. Demonstrated by Assisting God's People (vv. 25-26)—There could hardly be two more different people than Abraham and Rahab. One was a respected Hebrew patriarch while the other was a female Gentile. Abraham was a moral, admired leader; Rahab was a prostitute. However, the actions of both demonstrated that their faith was genuine.

The account of Rahab is found in Joshua 2:1-21. In Jericho she "received the messengers" Joshua had sent there as spies.

"By faith the prostitute Rahab, because she welcomed the spies, was not killed with those who were disobedient."
Hebrews 11:31, NIV

Notes

She confessed her faith in the Lord to the Hebrew spies and then risked her life by helping them to escape capture and return safely to their camp (Josh. 2:8-16). Rahab had declared her faith, and her works demonstrated that her faith was real. She later became a faithful member of the Hebrew nation and is named in Jesus' genealogy (Matt. 1:5). She also is listed as one of the pioneers of the faith (Heb. 11:31).

In 2:26 James completed his argument by restating his main point, "faith without works is dead." But here James compared "faith without works" to a "body without the spirit." "Spirit" has no definite article in the Greek text, so the word could mean "breath" as it often did in common usage. It could also refer to the vital spirit that animates the body.

This figure allowed James to repeat his point even more forcefully than before. A skilled spiritual coroner was not needed. Confidently, James placed workless faith on a cold slab and pronounced it dead. A living faith always shows its life by its deeds.

Several years ago a television news program showed a video of a large group of skydivers. The photographer who filmed this jump was an experienced skydiver. He had jumped from the plane along with numerous others in the group and filmed them as they floated through the air and then opened their parachutes.

The video went berserk just as the final skydiver opened his parachute. The announcer then reported the cameraman had fallen to his death, having jumped out of the plane without his parachute. He thought he was safe until he reached for the absent rip cord and realized his error. Tragically, he had acted with thoughtless haste and deadly presumption. Nothing could save him, for his faith was in a parachute he had never buckled on.

What evidence can we see in our lives that demonstrates we have placed our faith in the Lord Jesus Christ? Are our lifestyles particularly different from those of nonbelievers? Have we concluded that what we do doesn't really matter?

James did not teach that we can work our way to salvation and heaven. However, he clearly said works demonstrate salvation. He asked in effect, *If your faith doesn't work, what good is it?*

Have you had doubts about your salvation, your relationship with God? Maybe you are a good person—you have gone to church, you've known about Christ, you have read the Bible, you have attended Bible study classes—but you are not absolutely sure that if you died today, you would go to heaven. You can be sure. If you have not settled that issue, do so today. You may pray a prayer similar to this:

"Not everyone who says to Me, 'Lord, Lord!' will enter the kingdom of heaven, but only the one who does the will of My Father in heaven."
Matthew 7:21

Father in heaven, thank You for sending Your Son Jesus to die in my place, paying for my sins. I confess I am a sinner, and I invite Jesus into my heart and life to be my Lord and my Savior. Please save me right now, and help me become the person You created me to be. Thank You for answering my prayer.

Then tell your pastor, your group leader, or a Christian friend of your commitment to Christ. Publicly profess your faith in a Bible-believing church and obey the Lord's command to follow Him in baptism.

Seek to live for Him each day, trusting Him to pick you up when you fall, to forgive you, and to help you to walk in His paths (Ps. 119:105). The more you walk with Him, the deeper your assurance of salvation will become. Let your faith produce works.

Content Points

1. As the spirit gives life to the body, so works give life to faith.
2. If one's faith doesn't work, it is of little worth.
3. We can be sure of our salvation.
4. Good works are a by-product of walking with God and are initiated by Him.

Discussion Questions

1. Jesus told us the minimum entrance requirements to heaven (How little is required?). Do you think some Christians have that mind-set and thus do as little as they can?
2. Think about the relationship of Christians to society as a whole. Do most Christians really seem all that different from non-Christians?

Application Ideas

1. If it takes good works to give life to faith, which of these places does your faith most closely resemble:

Emergency room	Recovery room
Well-patient clinic	Intensive Care
Rehabilitation	Nursery
Other? ______________________________	

2. What has answering this question shown you about your faith?

Notes

SUMMARY

1. The teaching of Paul and James on faith and works is not contradictory, but complementary.

2. We can and should examine the genuineness of our faith in light of our works (2 Cor. 13:5).

3. Faith is more than religious talk or opinions. Real faith motivates believers to practical service rooted in love for God and people.

4. We are saved by faith alone, but not by faith that is alone. Genuine saving faith is accompanied by fruit.

5. We can be sure and assured of our salvation.

Going Deeper— The Theology of Paul and James

At first glance the theology of James and Paul may seem to be contradictory. Paul emphasized that a person "is justified by faith apart from works of law" (Rom. 3:28). He wrote in Ephesians 2:8-9: "For by grace you are saved through faith, and this is not from yourselves; it is God's gift—not from works, so that no one can boast."

Like James, however, Paul taught believers' good works demonstrated their faith: "For we are His creation—created in Christ Jesus for good works, which God prepared ahead of time so that we should walk in them" (Eph. 2:10).

James declared, "Faith, if it doesn't have works, is dead by itself" (Jas. 2:17). In 2:24 he added that we are "justified by works and not by faith alone." Paul and James, however, were not soldiers of different armies fighting against each other, but soldiers of the same army fighting back to back against enemies coming from opposite directions.[2]

Throughout his ministry to Gentiles, Paul had to confront a segment of Jewish Christians who insisted that to be saved Gentiles had to believe in Jesus plus practice Judaism. Paul's emphasis, therefore, was that salvation is by grace alone.

James, however, was fighting against a segment of professed believers who insisted that salvation by grace through faith brought absolute freedom to do as one pleased. Salvation was a free gift that brought no obligations. They ignored Jesus' warning in Matthew 7:21. In other words, genuine faith is expressed in godliness and service to others.

In summary: (1) Paul emphasized the root of our salvation, while James focused on the fruit after salvation. (2) Paul looked at life from God's perspective (in Christ we are righteous in God's sight), while James looked at life from a human perspective (in Christ we follow Him). (3) Paul used the term justified *in reference to the act of God at salvation while James used it to refer to validating or giving evidence of salvation.*

Going Deeper— The Genealogy of Jesus

The genealogy of Jesus as given in Matthew 1 was written to a Jewish audience. Matthew's intent was to show that Jesus was descended from the line of David. This proof enabled early believers to claim the Old Testament promise that there would always be an heir to David's throne (2 Sam. 7; Ps 132:11-12). The crowds often would use the term "Son of David" to call out to Jesus as he passed by.

The inclusion of the name of Rahab (v. 5) was unprecedented for two reasons. ***First,*** *genealogies of that day did not include the names of women. This pattern is clearly established in Genesis 5.*

Second*, one would assume that only women of great repute would be listed. Such is the name of Mary in Matthew 1:16. However, the inclusion of Rahab, a pagan prostitute, in Matthew 1:5 is remarkable. Rahab, who saved the lives of the spies in the city of Jericho, became a part of the Jewish nation and married into the tribe of Judah. She gave birth to Boaz who was the great grandfather of David.*

Equally stunning is the name of Tamar, who disguised her face and slept with her father-in-law Judah in order to bear an heir for her dead husband (Gen. 38). Another unlikely name is Ruth, a pagan widow who bore David's grandfather Boaz. Implied but not named is Bathsheba (Matt. 1:6), a victim of David's lust, who bore Solomon.

By using Rahab as a model of faith with works, James disregarded her shameful past and lifted her to the status of Abraham. Rahab is also mentioned in the heroes of faith chapter of Hebrews (Heb. 11:31). We learn from Rahab that it is not who you were but who you presently are that counts with God.

1. John Bisagno, *The Power of Positive Praying* (Grand Rapids, MI: Zondervan Publishing House, 1965) 24.
2. Paraphrase of Alexander Ross, "The Epistles of James and John," *The New International Commentary on the New Testament* (Grand Rapids, MI: William B. Eerdmans Publishing Company, 1954), 53.

JAMES 3:1-18 (HCSB)

*1Not many should become teachers, my brothers, knowing that
we will receive a stricter judgment; 2for we all stumble in many
ways. If anyone does not stumble in what he says, he is a mature
man who is also able to control his whole body.*

*3Now when we put bits into the mouths of horses to make
them obey us, we also guide the whole animal. 4And consider
ships: though very large and driven by fierce winds, they are
guided by a very small rudder wherever the will of the pilot
directs. 5So too, though the tongue is a small part of the body,
it boasts great things. Consider how large a forest a small fire
ignites. 6And the tongue is a fire. The tongue, a world of unrighteousness, is placed among the parts of our bodies; it pollutes the
whole body, sets the course of life on fire, and is set on fire by hell.*

*7For every creature—animal or bird, reptile or fish—is
tamed and has been tamed by man, 8but no man can tame the
tongue. It is a restless evil, full of deadly poison. 9With it we bless
our Lord and Father, and with it we curse men who are made
in God's likeness. 10Out of the same mouth come blessing and
cursing. My brothers, these things should not be this way. 11Does
a spring pour out sweet and bitter water from the same opening? 12Can a fig tree produce olives, my brothers, or a grapevine
produce figs? Neither can a saltwater spring yield fresh water.*

*13Who is wise and understanding among you? He should
show his works by good conduct with wisdom's gentleness. 14But
if you have bitter envy and selfish ambition in your heart, don't
brag and lie in defiance of the truth. 15Such wisdom does not
come down from above, but is earthly, sensual, demonic. 16For
where envy and selfish ambition exist, there is disorder and
every kind of evil. 17But the wisdom from above is first pure, then
peace-loving, gentle, compliant, full of mercy and good fruits,
without favoritism and hypocrisy. 18And the fruit of righteousness is sown in peace by those who make peace.*

Unit Three: Serve Others!

Lesson Five

SEEK POWER OVER YOURSELF, NOT OVER OTHERS (JAMES 3:1-18)

I. Beware of Seeking Control Through Teaching (3:1-2)

II. Be in Control of Your Speech (3:3-12)

A. Because of Words' Power (vv. 3-4)

B. Because of Words' Potential for Evil (vv. 5-8)

C. Because of Words' Possibilities (vv. 9-12)

III. Be Confident Godly Wisdom Controls Your Conduct (3:13-17)

A. The Demonstration of Godly Wisdom (v. 13)

B. The Description of Worldly Wisdom (vv. 14-16)

C. The Description of Godly Wisdom (v. 17)

IV. Be Assured You Will See Good Results (3:18)

LEARNING GOALS

As a result of studying this lesson, learners will:

- *Understand the responsibility and accountability of Christian teachers*
- *Appreciate the power of words and their potential for good and evil*
- *Explain the difference between the world's wisdom and God's wisdom*
- *Identify the kind of wisdom that shapes their lives*
- *Cite the outcomes of following the two kinds of wisdom*

In our study of James 2:14-26 we saw that real faith produces good works. How many kinds of "good works" are there? To this point James had only emphasized giving help to the poor (vv. 15-17), but words are works too. A person's words demonstrate either the presence or the absence of faith. Words can accomplish great good, and they can wreak horrible havoc. James already had cautioned believers to speak carefully (1:19,26). In chapter 3 he warned against the misuse of the tongue.

Some of us were born with a foot in our mouths—like the stock boy at the grocery store. A woman asked him, "Can I buy half a head of lettuce?" He walked back to ask the manager, not realizing she was walking right behind him. With a sneer he said to the manager, "You're not going to believe this, but there's an old bag out there who wants to buy half a head of lettuce." He turned, saw her standing there, and quickly added, "And this fine lady would like to buy the other half." Our mouths can get us into a lot of trouble.

Before taking a close look at James's message in chapter 3, let's affirm a couple of basic truths. First, the tongue is simply an organ of speech; it is operated by the heart, which in biblical terms includes our ability to reason, to feel, and to choose. James fully understood that.

He by no means intended his readers to think that sinful attitudes and opinions were acceptable as long they were not put into words (see 3:14). He was indicating that all too often our words reveal the sad spiritual state of our hearts.

Second, Galatians 5:16-26 makes clear that we believers still have an inward struggle with our sinful human nature. We can live in obedience to Christ only by yielding control to the indwelling Holy Spirit (to walk in the Spirit), and none of us do that with absolute consistency (see Jas. 3:2). Nevertheless, the only hope for controlling either our words or our deeds lies in our learning to rely on the Spirit to enable us to live in love and holiness.

Let's allow these two truths to illuminate our understanding of James 3.

[1]Not many should become teachers, my brothers, knowing that we will receive a stricter judgment; [2]for we all stumble in many ways. If anyone does not stumble in what he says, he is a mature man who is also able to control his whole body.

I. Beware of Seeking Control Through Teaching (vv. 1-2)

Evidently many of James's readers were seeking to become teachers in the church. James's command that "not many should become teachers" emphasizes the serious nature of seeking the office or role of teacher and its great responsibilities under God. "Teachers" could have included itinerant or traveling teachers who helped build a strong doctrinal foundation for new believers. The term certainly included spiritually gifted teachers in the church, the kind Paul mentioned in 1 Corinthians 12:28.

These official teachers in the local church helped church members to grow as disciples. In addition, Christian churches seem to have followed the pattern of Jewish synagogues in allowing visitors and others to speak to the congregation (Acts 13:13-16; 14:1-2; 1 Cor. 14:26-34). The church members had the privilege of sharing spiritual truth and insights during their gatherings.

Having the role of teacher gave a person high status, respect, and authority among believers. Seeing this, some evidently desired this office with impure motives. Others who sought this position did not have the spiritual gift of teaching.

James discouraged self-centered people from grabbing the spotlight and freely expressing half-baked opinions to others. He was aware that some unqualified and ungifted people coveted the attention and respect given to teachers.

Some folk simply love to hear themselves talk, even when they have nothing significant to say. The first-century church had problems not only with false prophets (2 Pet. 2:1) but also with unfit teachers. Churches face similar problems today.

To underscore the sense of the teachers' weighty responsibility, James explained why large numbers of Christians should hesitate to seek the office of teacher—"we will receive a stricter judgment" (Jas. 3:1). James used "we" (vv. 1,2,9), indicating that he himself was among those teachers who were liable to this "stricter judgment."

His readers already were well aware of this truth. Jesus had declared, "Much will be required of everyone who has been given much. And even more will be expected of the one who has been entrusted with more" (Luke 12:48).

Teaching in any sense is not a privilege to be lightly assumed. People always have been eager to hear new ideas, and sometimes they tragically accept erroneous opinions as valid. Teachers are required to teach the truth, not opinions. Christian teachers teach the gospel along with its instructions and implications for how to live. They themselves also must live up to God's requirements.

To fail to live by what they teach brings stricter judgment because of the greater influence they exert on others. God gives teachers a great responsibility and holds them accountable for how they carry it out.

Those who sought to be teachers may have assumed the remainder of chapter 3 was aimed at them. Notice, though, that James did not mention teachers after verse 1.

"[The teacher's and other leader's] responsibility is to equip God's people to do his work and build up the church, the body of Christ, until we come to such unity in our faith and knowledge of God's Son that we will be mature and full grown in the Lord, measuring up to the full stature of Christ."
Ephesians 4:12-13, NLT

Notes

His comments about the use of the tongue in verses 2-12 certainly applies to teachers, but more likely he intended a broader application ("we all," v. 2). Although teachers will be held to a stricter accountability, all of us are accountable to God for what we say. James used colorful instruction, subdued warnings, and pastoral pleas to urge all believers to stop using their tongues to hurt and control others.

James 3:2 says in essence that if you can control your mouth, you are mature. The Greek word translated "mature" sometimes is translated "perfect," but it also can carry the meaning of "mature" or "healthy." In verse 2 it cannot mean perfection in the sense of sinless living because, as James attested, "we all stumble," meaning we all sin. (See **Going Deeper—Mature,** p. 100.)

James warned that individuals are more likely to sin in what they say than in any other way. The person able to avoid stumbling in speech has demonstrated maturity in self-discipline. That kind of person "is able to control his whole body." One of the most difficult aspects of self-control is guarding what we say. A key part of becoming what God has called us to be in Christ is submitting our speech to God's control.

Content Points

1. There were three kinds of teachers in the early church:
   a. official teachers who instructed the new disciples
   b. traveling or itinerant teachers
   c. members of the body who desired to share
2. We should be careful in seeking any leadership position, asking ourselves:
   a. Am I doing this with right motives, or seeking something for myself?
   b. Am I qualified and gifted to serve in this capacity?
3. The speech that comes from our mouths is a good indicator of our spiritual maturity.

Discussion Questions

1. Why does God hold teachers to a higher standard than their students?
2. What does a believer's speech indicate about his or her spiritual maturity?

Application Ideas

1. Have you ever sought a leadership position in church? What were your motives?
2. Have you declined or even fought against taking a leadership position in church?
3. Have you used your God given talents to the best of your ability?

4. Has your service ever been a reflection of your self-interest rather than the interests of your church, others, or God?
5. Look at Ephesians 4:29 in the margin. Use this five-point test to guard your speech:
    - Is it wholesome?
    - Is it helpful?
    - Does it build others up or tear them down?
    - Does the person I am speaking to need to hear this?
    - Does it benefit the person I am speaking to and/or the person I'm speaking about?

"Do not let any unwholesome talk come
out of your mouths,
but only what is helpful
for building others up
according to their needs,
that it may benefit those who listen."
Ephesians 4:29, NIV

3Now when we put bits into the mouths of horses to make them obey
us, we also guide the whole animal. 4And consider ships: though
very large and driven by fierce winds, they are guided by a very
small rudder wherever the will of the pilot directs. 5So too, though
the tongue is a small part of the body, it boasts great things. Con-
sider how large a forest a small fire ignites. 6And the tongue is a fire.
The tongue, a world of unrighteousness, is placed among the parts
of our bodies; it pollutes the whole body, sets the course of life on
fire, and is set on fire by hell. 7For every creature—animal or bird,
reptile or fish—is tamed and has been tamed by man, 8but no man
can tame the tongue. It is a restless evil, full of deadly poison. 9With
it we bless our Lord and Father, and with it we curse men who are
made in God's likeness. 10Out of the same mouth come blessing and
cursing. My brothers, these things should not be this way. 11Does
a spring pour out sweet and bitter water from the same opening?
12Can a fig tree produce olives, my brothers, or a grapevine produce
figs? Neither can a saltwater spring yield fresh water.

II. *Be in Control of Your Speech* (vv. 3-12)

Our time in history has been described as the information and communication age. You can talk with people all around the world in a matter of seconds. Most of us have multiple conversations each day and spend a good bit of our time talking. We may speak thousands of words in a day. For any of us to speak that much while allowing God's Spirit to keep it all under control makes for no easy task. Did you ever wish you could take back something you said?

James's words stress the importance of controlling what we say because of words' power (vv. 3-4), words' potential for evil (vv. 5-8), and words' possibilities (vv. 9-12).

Notes

"There is one who speaks rashly, like a piercing sword; but the tongue of the wise brings healing." Proverbs 12:18

"The tongue that heals is a tree of life, but a devious tongue breaks the spirit." Proverbs 15:4

"Life and death are in the power of the tongue, and those who love it will eat its fruit." Proverbs 18:21

"The one who guards his mouth and tongue keeps himself out of trouble." Proverbs 21:23

[3]Now when we put bits into the mouths of horses to make them obey us, we also guide the whole animal. [4]And consider ships: though very large and driven by fierce winds, they are guided by a very small rudder wherever the will of the pilot directs.

A. Because of Words' Power (vv. 3-4)—We need to exercise tight control over our speech because of its power. The influence exerted by the tongue is way out of proportion to its size. To make that point James cited the way we control horses by putting relatively small "bits" into their mouths. When we tug at reins attached to the bits, we turn their heads and thereby direct their large, powerful bodies.

The word translated "bits" is the noun that comes from the verb meaning "to bridle." Although insignificant in size when compared to a horse, that small bit enables a rider to control even an unruly horse. James's illustration points to the great power exerted by such a small bit.

James used a second illustration to show the disproportionate power of the relatively tiny tongue. "Consider ships" is literally "Behold the ships!" James emphasized both the large size of the ships and the fact that they often were "driven by fierce winds." These vessels of James's day were small by modern standards, but the ship that took Paul to Rome accommodated 276 passengers (see Acts 27:37).

In spite of their size and the tumultuous weather they faced, those ships were "guided by a very small rudder" that was under the control "of the pilot." How marvelous that so large a vessel could be controlled by such a small rudder!

While both the bit and the rudder exert great power, they are under the control of a rider and a pilot respectively. The powerful tongue likewise needs to be under the control of one who walks in the Spirit. Like the bit and rudder, the tongue can exert a powerful influence. As we often have heard, silence is not always golden; sometimes it's yellow. Sweet silence in Christian fellowship, however, is better than acrid speech. James was not commending silence in preference to speech.

Ask yourself if you can answer no to each of these:

- Do you gossip and spread rumors?
- Do you criticize and tear others down?
- Do you talk about people behind their backs?
- Do you curse and use foul language?

[5]So too, though the tongue is a small part of the body, it boasts great things. Consider how large a forest a small fire ignites. [6]And the tongue is a fire. The tongue, a world of unrighteousness, is placed among the parts of our bodies; it pollutes the whole body, sets the

course of life on fire, and is set on fire by hell. [7]For every creature—animal or bird, reptile or fish—is tamed and has been tamed by man, [8]but no man can tame the tongue. It is a restless evil, full of deadly poison.

B. Because of Words' Potential for Evil (vv. 5-8)— "So too" introduces the application of James's two vivid illustrations. Indeed "the tongue is a small part of the body," yet this tiny member of the human body "boasts great things" (v. 5). We might have expected James to say the tongue "has great power" or "controls great things." The term for "boasts" in this context denotes an arrogant or even a threatening kind of boasting. Thus James was preparing the way for his comments on words' huge potential for evil.

Words can destroy a life or even thousands of lives overnight. How many people have ruined their marriages, their careers, their own or others' reputations, their churches, or their friendships with selfish, bitter, angry, or careless words? How has your life been damaged by someone's hurtful words? How have you hurt someone else with your words?

Many of us who would never even consider striking someone with our fists hardly hesitate to cut people with our sharp tongues. "Sticks and stones may break my bones, but words will never hurt me" is one of the great lies of childhood.

A tongue can express all kinds of sinful wickedness—idolatry, blasphemy, jealousy, greed, lust, and hatred. Evil speech also includes lying, manipulating, gossiping, complaining, bragging, putting others down, and profanity.

Verse 6 begins to stress the tongue's great potential for evil in the most extreme terms imaginable. The tongue is "a fire." Words can do terrible damage. Fire (and words) under control, however, can give welcomed warmth and light. Fire (and words) out of control can be devastating. A great forest can be set aflame by a small fire.

In 1983 in Australia, a fire destroyed miles and miles of land, villages, and livestock across two states. All of this destruction started with a single match. "The tongue is a fire" that can spark that kind of conflagration. The tongue's destruction includes "a world of unrighteousness … placed among the parts of our bodies," and it produces terrible consequences. "It pollutes the whole body, sets the course of life on fire, and is set on fire by hell."

James pictured all moral wrongdoing bundled into its own world and identified it as the tongue. A source of deadly moral infection, the tongue pollutes the whole body, contaminating the entire personality. The "course of life" literally is "the wheel of life," a way of referring to life from the cradle to the grave. A fire burning in the middle of a wooden wheel spreads from its spokes to the entire

"A lying tongue hates those it hurts, and a flattering mouth works ruin."
Proverbs 26:28, NIV

"Lord, set up a guard for my mouth; keep watch at the door of my lips"
Psalm 141:3.

circumference. The wicked influence of the tongue can affect every aspect of life.

The flaming tongue ruins everything. Those flames have their source in hell. "Hell" translates the word *Gehenna* (see **Going Deeper—Hell,** p. 101). Jesus used this word as a symbol for final judgment and eternal punishment (Mark 9:43,47). Satan attempts to use our tongues as instruments of pain and destruction. God's Spirit works in us to redeem our tongues and to use them as instruments of loving grace.

The human race has been able to "tame," to some extent, every species of animal life. The word for "tame" signifies "to subdue, to control." At creation God gave humanity dominion (rule) over every living creature in the sea, in the air, and on the earth (Gen. 1:28). James used both the present and perfect tenses of "tamed" to emphasize the continuing aspect of humanity's control over the animal world (Jas. 3:8).

1. Have you ever tried to tame your tongue with your own power?
2. What would be your strategy?
3. How long do you think it would take? weeks? months? years? a lifetime? never?

The tongue, however, resists being tamed. It "is a restless evil, full of deadly poison." To say the tongue is "a restless evil" means perversity can always break out at any moment. These words picture a wild animal pacing back and forth in its cage and desiring to escape. Although people can cage an animal, the tongue seeks to avoid confinement. It constantly slips out of control.

"Full of deadly poison" gives a serpent-like character to the tongue. James may have wanted his readers to view the tongue as a snake lying in wait and eager to inject its deadly venom at the first target of opportunity. Are you afraid of poisonous snakes? We'd better fear the tongue.

After vividly describing the destructive power of the tongue, James observed that no one can tame that small body part. However, the Greek text also has a word meaning "of men" (literally the phrase is "no one of men"). This word lets us hear James at least hinting that although human beings alone cannot subdue the tongue, they do not have to do it alone. Divine help makes it possible to tame the otherwise untameable.

[9]With it we bless our Lord and Father, and with it we curse men
who are made in God's likeness. [10]Out of the same mouth come
blessing and cursing. My brothers, these things should not be this
way. [11]Does a spring pour out sweet and bitter water from the same
opening? [12]Can a fig tree produce olives, my brothers, or a grapevine
produce figs? Neither can a saltwater spring yield fresh water.

C. **Because of Words' Possibilities (vv. 9-12)**—James's words in verses 9-12 point to some problems words can cause, but they also remind us of words' potential for good. Speech can achieve great results. Words can inspire a sports team to do its best. Words can encourage a war-battered people to persevere. Words can offer comfort, hope, joy, and instruction. James's words about the tongue's powerful influence highlight the possibilities of great achievement with the tongue. The highest use of our mouths offers praise to God.

The highest use of our mouths offers praise to God.

In verse 9 James addressed believers' inconsistency in the way they used their tongues. Once more he included himself ("we") among those who needed this reprimand. He saw a grave conflict in the way Christians could "bless our Lord and Father" and then turn around and "curse men."

Cursing here does not necessarily mean just profanity. "Curse" refers primarily to invoking evil on someone. Such cursing includes not only profanity but also angry verbal abuse and even less confrontational actions such as slander. It also means any sort of put-down or unkind label.

The verb "bless" when used in reference to God means "praise." Blessing God was an act Jews often repeated. For instance, when God was mentioned in conversations, someone immediately would say, "Blessed be He." But to "bless God" in worship or in daily conversation and afterward to curse people "who are made God's likeness" is to call in question the genuineness of the words of praise.

While God's likeness in human beings has been marred by sin, it has not been obliterated. This "likeness" is reflected to some degree in every person God created. In a sense, then, to curse the people God has made in His image is to curse the Creator Himself.

In verse 10 "my brothers" softens this reprimand a bit but does not remove its sting. Placing "blessing and cursing" together does not suggest simultaneous expressions. "Things should not be this way" means that blessing God at one time and cursing others at another are morally and spiritually incompatible.

James shifted his emphasis slightly in this verse and began to speak of the mouth instead of the tongue. Both are sources of speech, but changing the focus opened the door for a vivid metaphor in verse 11. As words pour from the mouth, water pours from a spring.

Alternately blessing God and cursing God's creation is against our nature, both physically and spiritually. Genuine faith produces what is natural to it. Thus James asked his readers, "Does a spring pour out sweet and bitter water from the same opening?" The obvious and expected answer was no. In Judea some springs gushed undrinkable salty or brackish water, while other springs produced drinkable water. No one spring, however, provided both kinds of water.

Notes

Verbal abusers who think they can praise God are practicing self-deception. Their two actions are spiritually incompatible. Their worship is seriously flawed. Their praises are not genuine, but their abuse is painfully real.

Verse 12 adds to the emphasis on consistency. The question about a fig tree producing olives and a grapevine producing figs clearly anticipates no for an answer. That impossibility can no more happen than a salt water spring can produce fresh water.

James did not directly state the application of these illustrations to human speech, but his meaning is clear. A person's speech (fruit) reveals what his or her heart (root) contains. When someone goes to the doctor and says, "I am not feeling good," one of the first things the doctor says is, "Stick out your tongue." The tongue often reveals what's going on inside a person. That is true not only physically but also spiritually.

Cursing others indicates a spiritual malady. Sinful people speak sinful words. Those who verbally or otherwise abuse others, especially those over whom they exert some kind of control, cannot genuinely praise God with hypocrisy. When we have a problem with our tongues, we really have a heart problem:

A harsh tongue shows an angry heart.
A negative tongue shows a fearful heart.
An overactive tongue shows an unsettled heart.
A boasting tongue shows an insecure heart.
A filthy tongue shows an impure heart.
A critical tongue shows a bitter heart.
An encouraging tongue shows a caring heart.
A gentle tongue shows a loving heart.
A truthful tongue shows an honest heart.

What is the solution when we have a heart problem? Jesus is the Great Physician who specializes in heart transplants. He also is the Healer of sick hearts and the Cleanser of dirty hearts. He pours God's love into our hearts (Rom. 5:5), a love that praises God and blesses others. Let us determine to speak only pure and wholesome words of blessing. Although we will stumble in the area of speech, we should try, with God's help, to consistently speak only what is good. May we be sensitive to possibilities of using words in helpful and redemptive ways.

Content Points

1. The tongue, which is one of the smallest parts of the body, yields power far beyond its size.
2. The tongue not only yields power but all kinds of evil.
3. The tongue is like a caged wild animal, restless for the opportunity to strike.
4. The venom of the tongue can hurt and even kill (relationships, self-esteem, and so forth).

5. Praising God and abusing people are spiritually incompatible.

Discussion Questions

1. How have you been hurt by careless words?
2. Can you describe a time when you saw words spread out of control like a fire?
3. Describe a time (without naming any names) when you knew something really "juicy" and there was great struggle within you as to whether or not to tell it. What did you do?
4. Why is it so hard to keep this *restless evil* to ourselves?

Application Ideas

1. Does a relationship in your life right now suffer because of your thoughtless or hurtful words? What do you need to do to bring healing to that relationship? Will you do it?
2. Think about your spouse, children, parents, neighbors, friends, co-workers, boss, and church members. In which of the following ways do you "curse" them?
   - Point out their faults, criticize, nit-pick
   - Slander, demean
   - Nag
   - Spread gossip and/or rumors
   - Name-calling, profanity
   - Angry attitudes
3. How do your attitude and speech need to change?
4. Describe a time (without naming any names) when you knew something really "juicy" and there was a great struggle within you as to whether or not to tell it.
   - Did you keep it to yourself?
   - Should you have?
   - How did you feel about your decision?
5. Look at Philippians 4:8 in the margin. Paul's check-list for our thoughts makes a good evaluation for our speech as well. Use this list to evaluate your speech:
   - Do you know it is true?
   - Does it bring honor to the person spoken about and to God?
   - Is it a fair (just) thing to say?
   - Is it pure of slander, gossip, fault-finding, and malice?
   - Does it portray the person, institution, or situation in the best possible light? (lovely)
   - Is it positive, not negative? (commendable)
   - Does it hold up the highest standards for imitation? (moral excellence)
   - Does it look for the best? (praise)

*"Finally brothers,
whatever is true,
whatever is honorable,
whatever is just,
whatever is pure,
whatever is lovely,
whatever is commendable—
if there is any moral excellence
and if there is any praise—
dwell on these things."*
Philippians 4:8

Notes

We exercise godly wisdom when we get along with other people. Our relationships show how wise we really are.

[13]Who is wise and understanding among you? He should show his
works by good conduct with wisdom's gentleness. [14]But if you have
bitter envy and selfish ambition in your heart, don't brag and
lie in defiance of the truth. [15]Such wisdom does not come down
from above, but is earthly, sensual, demonic. [16]For where envy
and selfish ambition exist, there is disorder and every kind of evil.
[17]But the wisdom from above is first pure, then peace-loving, gentle,
compliant, full of mercy and good fruits, without favoritism and
hypocrisy.

III. *Be Confident Godly Wisdom Controls Your Conduct* (vv. 13-17)

Many of the problems we have are because of so-called personality conflicts. We find difficulty in getting along with some people. When our relationships are bad, everything about life turns sour. We may have much money and many opportunities, but we are miserable. Learning how to apply godly wisdom in all our relationships is vital.

A. The Demonstration of Godly Wisdom (v. 13) —This verse begins the discussion of the two kinds of wisdom we Christians have to choose between as we live out our lives. This new subject could touch on the determination of some readers to become teachers (3:1), or it may flow from previous warnings about the use of the tongue. Either way, this section indicates that James was concerned about Christian fellowship among believers.

The question, "Who is wise and understanding among you?" does not imply that no wise people were among James's readers. Wisdom has more to do with character in relationships than it has to do with education and intelligence. We exercise godly wisdom when we get along with other people. Our relationships show how wise we really are.

While all believers are to act toward people with wisdom, the Greek word for "wise" can describe the practical wisdom a teacher needs in relating to learners. The word for "understanding" describes a person who is an expert in some field.

Before becoming a teacher who influences the views of others, believers need more than self-confidence and mastery of a subject. Potential teachers in the church need to prove they are qualified to be teachers. The crucial evidence is in the person's "works," that is, in the person's actions.

The works of wise and understanding people demonstrate "good conduct with wisdom's gentleness." This lets us know that we can do good things in the wrong way. Good conduct is wise when it is done with "gentleness." The word translated "gentleness" implies humility, a significant characteristic of the Christian life. Humility is the opposite of arrogance and self-assertiveness. A humble person puts others first and does not allow pride to destroy relationships. One who is humble promotes peace and unity in the church whereas one governed by pride and arrogance brings only conflict and division. Even good actions done in a spirit of self-assertion and arrogance negate all claims to godly wisdom.

Content Points

1. Wisdom has more to do with character in relationships than it has to do with education and intelligence.
2. A humble person puts others first and does not allow pride to destroy relationships.

Discussion Questions

1. Based on the comments in verse 13, describe how a person can do something good in the wrong way.
2. What are some examples of attitude, speech, and conduct that make you consider a person wise?
3. What would make you question a person's wisdom?

Application Ideas

1. Do you think others consider you wise? Why or why not?
2. Would you be characterized as humble or prideful?
3. What steps can you take to address the areas where you lack wisdom?
4. Think about people that you consider very wise. What can you learn from their examples?

[14]But if you have bitter envy and selfish ambition in your heart, don't brag and lie in defiance of the truth. [15]Such wisdom does not come down from above, but is earthly, sensual, demonic. [16]For where envy and selfish ambition exist, there is disorder and every kind of evil.

B. The Description of Worldly Wisdom (vv. 14-16)—These verses describe worldly wisdom as opposed to godly wisdom. Satan, "the god of this age" (2 Cor. 4:4), promotes his wisdom successfully in the world. James pulled no punches in denouncing it as ungodly wisdom.

Earthly wisdom is characterized by "bitter envy and selfish ambition." "Envy" in verse 14 comes from a Greek word that can refer to zeal, to having enthusiasm for something. The adjective "bitter," however, shows James used "envy" in a negative sense. "Selfish ambition" translates a single word that can be rendered also as "self-seeking" or "faction." James was warning against operating on the basis of a jealous, conniving, partisan, hostile spirit.

Notes

"The one who trusts in himself is a fool, but one who walks in wisdom will be safe." Proverbs 28:26

This earthly kind of wisdom permeates the world's culture. Popular sayings such as "it's a dog-eat-dog world," "the rat race," and "we're number one!" lead people to aspire to be the big dog, the fastest rat, and the winner. To achieve their goals they will do whatever is required, even if it is morally and ethically wrong and harms others. The only sin in worldly wisdom's view is getting caught.

Such attitudes in either church members or leaders always breed disruption in a congregation's fellowship. Sadly, some believers seem to take pride in running roughshod over people or in undermining their leaders to have their own way.

For example, a church leader worked against his pastor by criticizing his every move and encouraging others not to follow his leadership. This man was part of a small group that eventually caused the pastor to resign. The man later bragged that this was not the first preacher he had helped run off.

Another example is a manipulative pastor who proudly confided to a friend that he had succeeded in removing from leadership positions some of the most faithful church members because they had at times questioned his approach and methods.

James admonished all believers not to "brag" as though their self-centered attitudes or actions were right. Such boasting is "to lie in defiance of the truth." "Truth" is either the whole message of the gospel or the fact that they actually did possess arrogant and selfish intentions.

This wisdom of the world definitely does not come down "from above," that is from God (v. 15). It rather is "earthly, sensual, and demonic." "Earthly" implies character based on this world's motives and values, which include selfishness, greed, and a generally godless approach to life.

This worldly wisdom is also "sensual." This term translates a Greek word that means "soul." It refers to the physical life given to all living beings—animal and human alike. The term is distinct from the spiritual life received when one is born again by faith in Christ.

The unredeemed life of humanity, our sinful human nature, concerns itself with pleasing self, not God. This world's wisdom is "demonic" or devilish. Perhaps James had in mind the efforts of some to take control of churches as unclean spirits often took control of people (Mark 1:21-28).

"For" in verse 16 points to the reason James denounced worldly wisdom so strongly. He knew that wherever its self-centered arrogance controlled church leaders or members, disastrous results followed. Believers who think worldly wisdom should guide them always bring "disorder and every kind of evil" into their churches.

The word for "disorder" carries the ideas of "confusion, unruliness, or dissension." Demonic wisdom drives people apart. "Every evil thing" shows that nothing good ever comes through acting on a worldly wisdom that originates in hell.

Content Points

1. Worldly wisdom is self-seeking, factious, and hostile.
2. The fruit of worldly wisdom such as envy and selfish ambition are destructive to personal relationships and to church fellowship.

Discussion Questions

1. How does worldly wisdom show evidence of pride and conceit?
2. How have you seen self-centered motives bring division and disorder in a church?
3. What steps should the leadership of a church take to help safeguard the church body from self-centered, worldly people?

Application Ideas

1. What are some ways in which you are self-seeking? Is this attitude common among worldly people?
2. It's hard to think of anything we would do as "demonic," but if it is not "from heaven" (from God), then it is of this fallen world and demonic (v. 15).
3. What motives, desires, and attitudes do you have that are not from God?
4. Ask yourself these questions:
    - In conversation, what situations or people do I talk about in ungodly ways?
    - What habits and activities do I engage in that are not from God?
    - Can I recognize these things as "worldly"? as "demonic"?
    - Am I ready to confess them and forsake them?

[17]But the wisdom from above is first pure, then peace-loving, gentle, compliant, full of mercy and good fruits, without favoritism and hypocrisy.

C. The Description of Godly Wisdom (v. 17)—"But" introduces the contrast of godly wisdom to worldly wisdom (Jas. 3:15-16). James described the true "wisdom from above," heavenly wisdom, as "pure." It has no sinful attitudes or motives. To live by godly wisdom means acting morally, having spiritual integrity, and harboring no selfish attitudes or motives. Compare this description with the self-seeking characteristic of one who lives according to worldly wisdom. A pure person desires to serve God, not self. He or she is not defiled or unrighteous.

"Those who are peacemakers will plant seeds of peace and reap a harvest of goodness." James 3:18, NLT

Notes

"The fear of the LORD *teaches a man wisdom, and humility comes before honor."* Proverbs 15:33, NIV

Heavenly wisdom prompts people to be "peace-loving," desiring, promoting, and being governed by peace, seeking to dispel rivalries and factions in the church. In contrast to the divisive party spirit and rivalry of this world's wisdom, true wisdom promotes peace instead of strife. It does so because it is "gentle" and "compliant." "Gentle" is also translated as "reasonable, considerate, or courteous."

We are truly wise when we treat others and their views with respect. Wisdom also is reflected when we show grace and love to the undeserving. "Compliant" means "reasonable, approachable, and willing to be persuaded or yield one's own rights." A person who follows this wisdom is willing to defer to others when no serious moral or doctrinal issue is at stake.

Heavenly wisdom is "full of mercy and good fruits." "Mercy" refers to compassion shown toward those in need of help. "Good fruits" probably points to kind, helpful actions on behalf of the needy. Finally, heavenly wisdom is "without favoritism and hypocrisy."

James already had warned against showing favoritism (2:1). Heavenly wisdom does not show partiality or discriminate against anyone, actions that invariably lead to division and disharmony. The opposite of hypocrisy is sincerity, which promotes honest, open relationships among fellow believers.

"The wisdom from above" encourages people who receive it to act quite differently from those who follow worldly wisdom. Churches whose members act in godly wisdom bear a powerful and effective Christian witness to all who are deceived by the world's wisdom.

Each of us will do well to examine our own attitudes and actions and evaluate the extent to which we are following the wisdom that comes from God or the wisdom that comes from Satan. Many of us may find that we need to rededicate ourselves to God's ways.

Content Points

1. God's wisdom is pure wisdom (not corrupt).
2. To live by godly wisdom means acting morally, having spiritual integrity, and harboring no selfish attitudes or motives.

Discussion Questions

1. Why is it so much easier to live by the world's wisdom rather than God's wisdom?
2. What happens in churches where worldly wisdom is followed?
3. Describe a church that would thoroughly reflect God's wisdom in the attitudes, actions, and relationships of its members.

Application ideas

1. Think about the sentence, "A pure person desires to serve God, not self." Think of one aspect of life in which you need to desire to serve God, not self. What steps can you begin to take toward that purity?
2. Look at the comparison chart in the margin. Consider the attitudes and actions which show God's wisdom at work versus those that reveal worldly wisdom.
   - Which areas best describe you?
   - In which areas do you most need the help of the Holy Spirit?

18 And the fruit of righteousness is sown in peace by those who make peace.

IV. Be Assured You Will See Good Results (v. 18)

James concluded his discussion on godly wisdom by emphasizing "peace." Living in accord with heavenly wisdom results in peace as opposed to the disorder of false wisdom. "Those who make peace" are the ones who live in peace with others and who promote peace among other people. God, the Author of peace, calls peacemakers His "children" (Matt. 5:9). Peacemakers who work at promoting peace raise a harvest of "righteousness."

"Righteousness" here refers to "right conduct that is pleasing to God, actions that conform to His will." Such righteousness will flourish in a setting of peace. Churches characterized by heavenly wisdom enjoy peace, unity, and conformity to Christ.

If we are at peace with others, we will act wisely toward them. We will not rub it in when they are hurt—we will help them rub it out. We will not hold over their heads some hurt they have done to us—we will forgive it. When somebody stumbles, we won't judge them—we will encourage them. We will neither emphasize their failures nor pretend we ourselves have no weaknesses.

If we are wise, we will not broadcast others' mistakes, belittle their suggestions, become insensitive to their feelings, or antagonize them to anger. We sow "in peace" when we act with loving-kindness toward others.

James 3:1-18 instructs us to demonstrate heavenly wisdom through our speech and describes the characteristics of such wisdom. We use constructive words and demonstrate heavenly wisdom when what we say promotes purity, peace, consideration, mercy, impartiality, and sincerity.

James 3:17

God's Wisdom	Worldly Wisdom
pure God-seeking moral spiritual	corrupt self-seeking defiled unrighteous
peace-loving reconciling bridge-building	factious devisive full of strife
gentle considerate courteous	harsh rude
compliant submissive yielding	rigid demanding unyielding
full of mercy giving compassionate	uncaring unhelpful self-centered
good fruits good works helpful	unfruitful bad fruit
impartial fair	biased, partial discriminates plays favorites
sincere not hypocritical genuine	insincere hypocritical disingenuous

Notes

"Blessed are the peacemakers, because they will be called sons of God." Matthew 5:9

We must pursue what promotes peace and what builds up one another." Romans 14:19

Do to others as you would have them do to you." Luke 6:31, NIV

"Love does no wrong to a neighbor." Romans 13:10a

"Make every effort to keep the unity of the Spirit through the bond of peace." Ephesians 4:3, NIV

"Above all, put on love—the perfect bond of unity." Colossians 3:14

As we saw in James 1:5, wisdom is a gift from God, and He gives it generously to those who ask. Ask Him today. He loves to give.

Content Points

1. Living by God's wisdom results in peace. Contrast this peace with the disorder and evil found by following the world's wisdom.
2. God has called us to be peacemakers (Matt. 5:9).
3. "Righteousness" is right conduct that pleases God.

Discussion Questions

1. Think about a time and place that you considered "peaceful." Why was it peaceful?
2. How did the peace occur?
3. How can we be peacemakers in our churches?
4. How does an environment of "peace" lead to "righteousness"?

Application Ideas

1. Which of your personal relationships need more peace?
2. How would your attitudes, speech, and actions need to change for there to be more peace in your relationships?
3. How can you be more of a peacemaker in your church?

SUMMARY

1. **God gives teachers a great responsibility and holds them accountable for how they carry it out.**

2. **Teachers must teach the truth, not opinions; they must live by what they teach.**

3. **The tongue holds great power, far beyond what its size would suggest. Our words can hurt and destroy in an instant, setting one's world aflame.**

3. **The world's wisdom is self-centered and self-seeking. God's wisdom is pure and seeks the best for others.**

4. **Worldly wisdom sows discord and strife. Godly wisdom sows peace and righteousness.**

[2]for we all stumble in many ways. If anyone does not stumble in what he says, he is a mature man who is also able to control his whole body.

Going Deeper—Mature (3:2)

The Greek term teleios *is translated "mature" in James 3:2. It can be translated "perfect," but it does not mean sinless. No one on earth—except Jesus—has ever attained that level of moral perfection. Rather, the term "perfect" in the context of "we all stumble" means "mature" or "complete." A mature Christian is a follower of Christ who is making progress toward the goal of becoming like Him.*

Some other examples of the use of this word to mean "mature" are as follows: Paul admonished the Corinthians to quit thinking as children but rather as adults (teleios), *meaning to demonstrate maturity in their thinking (1 Cor. 14:20).*

The goal of church leaders is to equip believers so that they are mature (teleios) *and not spiritual infants (Eph. 4:13). The mature* (teleios) *will realize that they have not yet attained everything God wants them to be, but they will press on toward the goal (Phil. 3:15).*

The prayer of Epaphras was that the Colossian believers would become mature (teleios) *believers, fully assured in their faith (Col. 4:12). Solid food or the deeper doctrines of the faith are for the mature* (teleios) *rather than for infants (Heb. 5:14).*

6 And the tongue is a fire. The tongue, a world of unrighteousness, is placed among the parts of our bodies; it pollutes the whole body, sets the course of life on fire, and is set on fire by hell.

Going Deeper—"Hell" (3:6)

The word "hell" translates Gehenna, *literally "the valley of Hinnom." This deep, narrow valley was located south of Jerusalem's walls.* Gehenna *occurs in Matthew 5:22,29-30; 10:28; 18:9; 23:15,33; Mark 9:43,45,47; Luke 12:5; and James 3:6. All of these references designate the place of eternal punishment of the wicked, generally in connection with the final judgment. It is associated with fire as the source of torment.*

"The valley of Hinnom" became the technical designation for the place of final punishment for two reasons. ***First,*** *the valley had been desecrated by the worship of Moloch, during which children had been offered as burnt offerings (Jer. 2:23; 7:31; 2 Chron. 28:3; 33:6).* ***Second,*** *because of those pagan and tragic practices the place was formally defiled by King Josiah (2 Kings 23:10).*

As a consequence the valley became associated in prophecy with the judgment to be visited upon the people (Jer. 7:32). Because it became the city's garbage dump and was continually burning the waste, the name became synonymous with both the worst defilement and the worst punishment.

JAMES 4:1-17 (HCSB)

*1What is the source of the wars and the fights among you? Don't
they come from the cravings that are at war within you? 2You
desire and do not have. You murder and covet and cannot
obtain. You fight and war. You do not have because you do not
ask. 3You ask and don't receive because you ask wrongly, so that
you may spend it on your desires for pleasure.*

*4Adulteresses! Do you not know that friendship with the
world is hostility toward God? So whoever wants to be the
world's friend becomes God's enemy. 5Or do you think it's withou
reason the Scripture says that the Spirit He has caused to live in
us yearns jealously?*

6But He gives greater grace. Therefore He says:

God resists the proud,
but gives grace to the humble.

*7Therefore, submit to God. But resist the Devil, and he
will flee from you. 8Draw near to God, and He will draw near
to you. Cleanse your hands, sinners, and purify your hearts,
double-minded people! 9Be miserable and mourn and weep.
Your laughter must change to mourning and your joy to sorrow.
10Humble yourselves before the Lord, and He will exalt you.*

*11Don't criticize one another, brothers. He who criticizes a
brother or judges his brother criticizes the law and judges the
law. But if you judge the law, you are not a doer of the law but a
judge. 12There is one lawgiver and judge who is able to save and
to destroy. But who are you to judge your neighbor?*

*13Come now, you who say, "Today or tomorrow we will travel
to such and such a city and spend a year there and do business
and make a profit." 14You don't even know what tomorrow will
bring—what your life will be! For you are a bit of smoke that
appears for a little while, then vanishes.*

*15Instead, you should say, "If the Lord wills, we will live and
do this or that." 16But as it is, you boast in your arrogance. All
such boasting is evil. 17So, for the person who knows to do good
and doesn't do it, it is a sin.*

Unit Three: Serve Others!

Lesson Six

SEEK WHAT IS BEST FOR OTHERS, NOT FOR YOURSELF (JAMES 4:1-17)

I. Eliminate Sources of Conflict (4:1-5)

A. The Craving to Possess (v. 2)
B. The Craving for Self-sufficiency (vv. 2-3)
C. The Craving for the World's Friendship (vv. 4-5)

II. Exhibit Humble Submission To God (4:6-12)

A. Submit to God (v. 7)
B. Resist the Enemy (v. 7)
C. Draw Near to God (v. 8)
D. Cleanse Hands and Purify Hearts (vv. 8-10)
E. Let God Be the Judge (vv. 11-12)

III. Emphasize God's Will (4:13-17)

A. Acknowledge the Uncertainty of Life (vv. 13-14)
B. Include God in All Planning (vv. 15-16)
C. Do Good (v. 17)

LEARNING GOALS FOR THIS LESSON

As a result of studying this lesson, learners will:

- *Identify three cravings that bring us into conflict with others*
- *Describe the relationship between submitting to God and resisting the Devil*
- *Explain the role of repentance in drawing near to God*
- *Understand the folly and sin in judging others*
- *Find security in seeking God's will in all aspects of life*

Notes

Someone said that the history of humanity can be traced more easily by its wars than by its accomplishments. That is a sad commentary, but it hits pretty close to home. Even sadder is the parallel in biblical history. Operating out of self-centered motives frequently has caused conflict within the community of faith:

- Lot could not get along with Abraham.
- Absalom led a rebellion against his father David.
- The disciples argued over greatness in the kingdom.
- The Corinthians fought regarding spiritual gifts.
- The Galatians were biting and devouring one another.
- The Ephesians warred regarding spiritual unity.
- Two women in the church at Philippi were told to live in harmony with each other.
- Paul had a face-to-face confrontation with Peter.
- James described church conflicts in terms of warfare.

In today's world some churches are better known for their internal friction than for their ministry in Christ's name. Acting according to the flesh rather than the Spirit presents a message contrary to the gospel. Jesus said, "By this all people will know that you are My disciples, if you have love for one another" (John 13:35). Hostile internal bickering damages a church's witness far more than external opposition.

James chose not to deal directly with particular problems, probably because both he and his readers knew what they were. Instead James identified and urged vital spiritual changes that could cool existing animosity whatever its root cause. Because this problem continues, his message has ageless value.

[1]What is the source of the wars and the fights among you? Don't they come from the cravings that are at war within you? [2]You desire and do not have. You murder and covet and cannot obtain. You fight and war. You do not have because you do not ask. [3]You ask and don't receive because you ask wrongly, so that you may spend it on your desires for pleasure. [4]Adulteresses! Do you not know that friendship with the world is hostility toward God? So whoever wants to be the world's friend becomes God's enemy. [5]Or do you think it's without reason the Scripture says that the Spirit He has caused to live in us yearns jealously?

I. *Eliminate Sources of Conflict* (4:1-5)

All of us have to wrestle with our selfish, sinful human nature and its attraction to the ways of the world. Our human nature leads us to seek whatever will give us power, prominence, and popularity. James identified three worldly cravings as sources of church conflict.

²You desire and do not have. You murder and covet and cannot obtain. You fight and war. You do not have because you do not ask.

A. The craving to possess (v. 2)—Could James really have been describing the actions of Christians in terms like *war, fight,* and *murder*? Afraid so. "Among you" in verse 1 makes clear that these verses continue to address believers.

Using words from the battlefield, James called church disputes "wars" and "fights." "Wars" translates a Greek word used to describe the totality of war, such as World War II. "Fights" refers to specific battles within the larger war. These were the separate disagreements or incidents that kept the divisive conflict going. James most likely described any kind of open hostility—verbal arguments, feuds, and the like—although actual physical conflict might have occurred.

James asked pointed questions and immediately plowed ahead to answer them himself. He identified one source as being "cravings that are at war within you." "Cravings" describes what drives people who are focused on their own pleasure, enjoyment, and satisfaction. The English word *hedonism* derives from this Greek term. The philosophy of hedonism views pleasure as the chief goal of life.

"But put on the Lord Jesus Christ, and make no plans to satisfy the fleshly desires." Romans 13:14

"Now those who belong to Christ Jesus have crucified the flesh with its passions and desires." Galatians 5:24

A large part of pleasure is having things go our way. We want people to agree with us and to follow our advice about what and how to do things. They, of course, have a similar desire; so to get our way we try to persuade them. We might resort to manipulation, intimidation, deceit, or some similar strategy. When we make pleasing ourselves our top priority, fights and quarrels inevitably result.

The text says these cravings are warring "within you," literally "in your members." "Members" refers basically to the parts of the human body, but the word sometimes indicates "members" of the church (1 Cor. 12:27). Some scholars hear James saying these cravings were within the church fellowship. People were taking sides against one another in their concern to have church affairs conform to their opinions. No doubt that was happening then, and it happens now.

These conflicts occur because of the cravings for pleasing ourselves that are "at war within" individual believers' hearts, as we all know from personal experience ("envy and selfish ambition in your heart," Jas. 3:14). Only by God's grace and through submitting to the enabling power of the Holy Spirit can we win these spiritual battles—"Walk by the Spirit and you will not carry out the desire of the flesh" (Gal. 5:16).

Accumulating certain possessions (think "new car fever") also pleases us. Scripture affirms that God created all things for us to enjoy and use. Too often, we love things and use people. We should love people and use things. An uncontrolled desire to possess can lead us to an obsessive

Too often we love things and use people. We should love people and use things.

Notes

"But those who want to be rich fall into temptation, a trap, and many foolish and harmful desires, which plunge people into ruin and destruction."
1 Timothy 6:9

lust for things and a gnawing envy of others who have those things. The way is paved for conflict.

For example, how much discord in the modern family can be traced to the craving for possessions? A widow died, leaving her house and its possessions to her two children. The two could not agree on who should take which furnishings. While one was out of town, the other had all the contents moved to his home in another state. This action resulted in a bitter rift between the siblings that took decades to bridge. How easily we can forget that relationships are infinitely more important than possessions!

James explained that "you desire" (a burning desire for something) and "you do not have" showed the futility of the desire, which remained unfulfilled. When we live principally to please ourselves, we also live with disappointment.

How are we to understand James's saying believers committed "murder" to get what they wanted? Was he using "murder" in a literal or a figurative sense? Scholars have proposed several options on this issue. Those who view murder as literal point to the Zealot background of some Jewish Christians. They might have retained the Zealots' belief in murder as an acceptable way to attain goals.

Others believe James was speaking conditionally—"If you choose pleasure instead of God, your craving could lead to murder." Other interpreters connect "murder" with "covet" as a figure of speech for the idea "you murderously covet."

Others simply see "murder" as a hyperbole, an exaggeration to make the point that envy gives birth to bitter resentment and hatred. "Everyone who hates his brother is a murderer" (1 John 3:15). This verse might be the best way to take James's meaning.

Even misguided believers' most violent, envy-fueled efforts prove fruitless; they fail to gain the position or thing they wanted. Undaunted, they charge ahead on the course they have chosen—"You fight and war." "Fight and war" are the verbal forms of the nouns found in James 4:1, but in reverse order.

The lack of peace in congregations and peoples' hearts is reflected in unrighteous behavior (read again Jas. 3:18). May God help all of us to learn the lesson shared by a senior adult: "The best thing I have learned to do is happily to do without."

Content Points

1. The desire to please ourselves results in conflict and fights with others.
2. Sinful human desires to have things our way also result in church conflicts.
3. Selfish desire for possessions and "things" often leads to the mistreatment of others.

Discussioin Questions
1. What common events in churches cause conflict?
2. What is the danger of happiness being the "highest good"? How does pursuing happiness create conflict?
3. Name some danger signs that indicate we are too wrapped up in "things."
4. How can selfish desires "murder" someone?

Application Ideas
1. Has your pursuit of happiness ever caused conflict or hurt someone else?
2. Have you ever been caught in a "church war"? Looking back, can you see how personal agendas played a part in the conflict?
3. Did you serve as an ambassador of peace in that conflict?

2You desire and do not have. You murder and covet and cannot obtain. You fight and war. You do not have because you do not ask.
3You ask and don't receive because you ask wrongly, so that you may spend it on your desires for pleasure.

B. The craving for self-sufficiency (vv. 2-3)—James explained further why selfish cravings aren't fulfilled. "You do not have because you do not ask" (v. 2). Instead of looking to God for provision in prayer, we seek to fill our needs in the same way nonbelievers do.

What hinders us from bringing our requests to God in prayer? Perhaps the reason that underlies all others is the deep-seated desire of sinful human nature to be independent of God. Somehow we keep trying to convince ourselves that we can be self-sufficient and that this is the better way to live.

How easily we can forget just how much we need God! If we were more dependent on Him and confessed our need for Him more, we'd pray more, worry less, and enjoy a deeper peace. We, as well as James's readers might protest, *But we do pray; God just does not answer our prayers.* James explained in verse 3 the reason many prayers are not answered. We do "not receive" because we ask "wrongly." The wrong is in petitioning God with self-centered motives.

"Now this is the confidence we have before Him: whenever we ask anything according to His will, He hears us."
1 John 5:14

Specifically James cited the intent to "spend" what we receive on our "desires for pleasure." "Spend" here means "squander," as it does in Luke 15:14's description of the prodigal's wasting all of his inheritance on selfish pursuits. "Pleasure" is the same word translated "cravings" (Jas. 4:1).

How often we view prayer as a means of obtaining what will give us pleasure! We want to feel good. We want to be comfortable. We want to have our senses satisfied. It's not wrong to enjoy life; but when pleasure becomes our number one goal, we are opening the door for discord within

Notes

"Do not love the world or the things that belong to the world. If anyone loves the world, love for the Father is not in him. For everything that belongs to the world—the lust of the flesh, the lust of the eyes, and the pride in one's lifestyle—is not from the Father, but is from the world. And the world with its lust is passing away, but the one who does God's will remains forever."
1 John 2:15-17

"Don't worry about anything, but in everything, through prayer and petition with thanksgiving, let your requests be made known to God."
Philippians 4:6

"And the peace of God, which surpasses every thought, will guard your hearts and your minds in Christ Jesus."
Philippians 4:7

"Take delight in the LORD, and He will give you your heart's desires."
Psalm 37:4

"He satisfies you with goodness."
Psalm 103:5a

"Whom do I have in heaven but You? And I desire nothing on earth but You."
Psalm 73:25

I gravitate toward minimalism when it comes to obedience. My default is, *What's the least I'm required to do and the most I can get away with?"*[1]

ourselves and with others. The purpose of prayer is not self indulgence, and God does not answer positively self-centered requests (see Matt. 6:10; 1 John 5:14-15).

God has promised to meet all our needs as we seek to make Him and His righteousness our top priorities (Matt. 6:33). We have every right as His children to expect He will keep His promises. Unfortunately, our materialistic culture has invaded our hearts, blurring the line between genuine needs and self-gratifying wants.

Content Points

1. Self-centeredness leads to prayerlessness.
2. Wrong motives in prayer lead to unanswered prayer.
3. God has promised to meet all our needs as we seek to make Him and His righteousness our top priorities, and not our own selfish desires.

Discussioin Questions

1. Philippians 4:6 tells us not to worry about anything and pray about everything. Why do you think most of us worry about everything and don't pray about anything?
2. Now look at Philippians 4:7. What is the result of getting the equation straight in verse 6?
3. What are some ways we pray with wrong motives?
4. What are common "wants" that we often call "needs"?

Application Ideas

1. Are you trusting God with your doubts, fears, struggles and relationships, as well as your material needs?
2. Are you seeking God's wisdom and will, or do you often have impure motives in prayer?
3. Think about the "wants" that you refer to as "needs." Do you find satisfaction in God alone? Read the verses from the Psalms in the margin.
4. Do you confess your wrong priorities to God and find true happiness in Him?

[4]Adulteresses! Do you not know that friendship with the world is hostility toward God? So whoever wants to be the world's friend becomes God's enemy. [5]Or do you think it's without reason the Scripture says that the Spirit He has caused to live in us yearns jealously?

C. The craving for the world's friendship (vv. 4-5)—This passage describes our spiritual condition when we are driven by a desire to be friends with the world. The goal of the Christian life is not seeing how close we can walk to the edge of worldliness without committing sin. The goal rather is to see how close we can walk with God and how far we can stay away from the world's sinful ways.

Many adults accept the behavior of little children who do daring things to impress them and gain approval. God, however, does not approve close-to-the-edge behavior from His children. Such behavior is unacceptable for a mature, devoted follower of Christ.

Verse 4 begins with a jolt—"Adulteresses!" The use of the feminine form suggests James used the term metaphorically. Examining ancient Greek texts reveals that some scribes, probably taking the word literally, balanced it by adding the masculine "adulterers" (see KJV). In the Old Testament God was viewed metaphorically as the Husband of Israel, so Israelites who turned to idols were said to have committed spiritual adultery.

By the time of James, the church (as the new Israel) already was being thought of as the bride of Christ (see 2 Cor. 11:2). In light of believers' self-centered worldliness, James accused them of spiritual adultery, of being unfaithful to the Lord Jesus Christ.

Spiritual adultery results from wanting "to be the world's friend." That kind of friendship makes us "God's enemy." Like a woman choosing between two suitors, each of us has to make a choice. We can move toward the seductive and pleasurable ways of the world, or we can follow the Lord who has demonstrated His immeasurable, selfless, sacrificial love for us.

The Greek text of verse 5 presents a couple of tough questions to translators, so we need not be surprised that different versions of the Bible show wide variations. The original text has no capital letters. Thus the first question relates to the subject of the verb "yearns"—"the Spirit He has caused to live in us yearns jealously." Is it "Spirit" (HCSB, NASB, meaning God's Spirit, that is, the Holy Spirit); or should it be "spirit" (KJV, NIV, meaning the human spirit)?

If the subject is the human spirit, the reading could be, "Or do you think Scripture says without reason that the spirit He caused to live in us envies [yearns] intensely?" In this case the passage would mean that human beings who choose to be this world's friends are virtually at the mercy of their inborn selfish inclinations. Only those who follow the instructions in verses 6-10 will be delivered from their own destructive tendencies.

If the subject is the Holy Spirit, the Greek can be understood in two ways. (1) It can mean the Holy Spirit does not produce our sinful envious yearnings. Thus James would be giving his readers authority ("Scripture says," v. 5) for his point that friendship with the world makes one an enemy of God. (2) It can be translated as in the Holman CSB, meaning that God's Spirit yearns jealously for His people's absolute commitment to Him. In light of the context, the translation "Spirit" with this second meaning seems the best fit.

"

"They have committed adultery, and blood is on their hands; they have committed adultery with their idols." Ezekiel 23:37

"I am jealous over you with a godly jealousy, because I have promised you in marriage to one husband—to present a pure virgin to Christ. But I fear that, as the serpent deceived Eve by his cunning, your minds may be corrupted from a complete and pure devotion to Christ." 2 Corinthians 11:2-3

Notes

"You are to never bow down to another god because the LORD, being jealous by nature, is a jealous God." Exodus 34:14

"For the LORD your God is a consuming fire, a jealous God." Deuteronomy 4:24

The second question relates to James's statement, "Scripture says" (Jas. 4:5). No single Old Testament verse corresponds exactly to the following wording, but many Old Testament passages teach God is a jealous God who will tolerate no rivals and who demands total, undivided loyalty (see Ex. 34:14). Perhaps the best answer is simply that James summarized these passages to challenge his readers to be faithful to God rather than to be friends of the world.

Scripture does not speak "without reason," meaning "to no purpose or in vain." We need to carefully observe all of the warnings and instructions God has given us. To fail to do so puts us in the position of "God's enemy."

Content Points

1. The Christian life is to walk as closely as possible with God and as far away as possible from the world.
2. Living in the world while professing to follow Christ is spiritual adultery.
3. Being the "world's friend" means being "God's enemy."
4. The Holy Spirit living in every believer jealously yearns for our lives to be committed to Christ, not the world.

Discussioin Questions

1. What are some examples of "spiritual adultery"?
2. What activities, attitudes, or habits make us God's enemy?
3. In the Bible God is described as "jealous." When might it be right for us to be jealous?

Application Ideas

Think about sexual adultery as being "divided in heart" toward the one for whom you have professed an undivided commitment. As a Christian, you have made a promise. Do the things of the world ever steal your heart from full commitment to Christ? Are you a spiritual adulterer? If so, will you "renew your vows" today?

A Spiritual Wedding Vow:

Dear Jesus,
I take you to be my Lord,
I promise to honor, to love,
and to cherish you alone
in sickness as in health,
in poverty as in wealth,
in hardship as in blessing,
until death alone shall unite us.

[6]But He gives greater grace. Therefore He says:
God resists the proud,
but gives grace to the humble.
[7]Therefore, submit to God. But resist the Devil, and he will flee from
you. [8]Draw near to God, and He will draw near to you. Cleanse
your hands, sinners, and purify your hearts, double-minded people!
[9]Be miserable and mourn and weep. Your laughter must change to
mourning and your joy to sorrow. [10]Humble yourselves before the
Lord, and He will exalt you. [11]Don't criticize one another, brothers.
He who criticizes a brother or judges his brother criticizes the law
and judges the law. But if you judge the law, you are not a doer of
the law but a judge. [12]There is one lawgiver and judge who is able to
save and to destroy. But who are you to judge your neighbor?

II. Exhibit Humble Submission to God (4:6-12)

But" in verse 6 emphasizes that we have hope in our difficult and ongoing spiritual fight against envy. Envy has its source in our deep-seated, self-centered pride. Arrogant pride not only causes conflicts in our relationships with other people but also in our relationship with God. Since pride is the primary cause of conflicts, what is the cure?

The antidote for poisonous pride is humility—"But He gives greater grace. Therefore He says, 'God resists the proud, but gives grace to the humble'" (Jas. 4:6). God gives greater grace to us when we face greater needs. God's grace—readily available—helps us overcome our weaknesses.

"He says" affirms that God speaks through the Scriptures. Listening to Him by regularly exposing ourselves to His Word is essential to spiritual vitality and growth. James then quoted Proverbs 3:34 from the Greek translation of the Old Testament.

This proverb begins, "God resists the proud." He is permanently set against those who presumptuously believe they are better than others and deserve more than others; therefore, they mean to get on top and stay there at any cost. God has declared war on self-centeredness. Have you noticed that God has a unique way of using life's circumstances to deal with our pride? If we are legitimate children of the Father, He will deal with the issue of pride in our lives.

"But," the proverb continues, He "gives grace to the humble." The only way we can experience God's grace is through humility. He doesn't give grace to people who are full of pride and self-sufficiency. He wants us to confess, "God, I need your help." When we are ready to humbly receive God's help, He grants "grace to help us at the proper time" (Heb. 4:16, KJV).

"Grace, grace, God's grace,
Grace that will pardon
and cleanse within;
Grace, grace, God's grace,
Grace that is greater than
all our sin."[2]

Notes

Do you know of ways pride hinders you from being more what God wants you to be? Think about your attitudes, your marriage, your family, your vocational relationships, and your friendships. What difference would a good dose of humility make? Only as we humble ourselves in the presence of the living God will He give us grace to make possible our becoming more of what He desires us to be. He will work in our lives to make the changes we cannot make on our own.

The next few verses give five specific and practical actions to enable us to experience God's help and guidance in our spiritual struggles. Remember, humility is the starting point.

Content Points

1. Envy is birthed in our deep-seated, self-centered pride.
2. Pride is the source of most conflicts.
3. The antidote to pride is humility.
4. Only God gives us victory over pride through humility.

Discussioin Questions

1. Why does pride block our relationship with God?
2. Why is it difficult to be humble?
3. How does God use life's circumstances to teach us humility?

Application Ideas

1. In what areas do you struggle with pride? Are you aware of how this hurts your relationship with others? Of how this hurts your relationship with God?
2. Will you commit to pray daily for God to teach you humility in these areas?

[7]Therefore, submit to God. But resist the Devil, and he will flee from you.

A. "Submit to God" (v. 7)—"Submit" calls for more than obedience. It means "to subject oneself." It means "the proud" and all others should decide once and for all to be under God's authority, to let God be Lord in our lives, to give Him control, and to quit trying to do as we choose. Instead, we must choose to do as He directs.

As we saw in 4:1, conflict with others results from conflict within. When we can't get along with other people, generally we are experiencing civil war in our hearts. The starting point for peace with others is peace within.

That peace is found in allowing Christ to rule in our hearts. When we have His peace in our hearts, we'll be at peace with other people. Without His peace, we are far more likely to try to manipulate and control others so we can have our way.

Content Points

1. We are to be subject in obedience to God as our Lord.
2. Living in peace with Christ, and with His peace in us, brings us into peace in our relationships with others.

Discussioin Questions

1. We all want to "call the shots" in life. How can we learn to let God have control moment by moment?
2. What is the difference between having "peace with Christ" through salvation and living in the "peace of Christ" in our daily lives?
3. How would living in Christ's peace help you live in peace with others?

Application Ideas

1. List areas where you live in doubt, fear, struggle, and worry.
2. List conflicts you have with other people.
3. Begin to pray over these lists and commit them to God. Ask for His help to overcome them. Pray for victory and for the peace of Christ in your heart and relationships.

"Let the peace of Christ rule in your hearts." Colossians 3:15, NIV

[7]Therefore, submit to God. But resist the Devil, and he will flee from you.

B. "Resist the Devil" (v. 7)—"But" suggests that we are not ever to submit to "the Devil." The Greek word for "resist" is a military term. It means "to take a stand against" or to 'withstand an attack." When we submit ourselves to God, His powerful grace enables us to "resist the Devil," that is, to stand against him rather than to be bowled over by him. This resistance is possible only through the strength God's grace provides as we submit to Him.

On our own, we cannot win against the Devil. When we resist the Devil in the Lord's strength, he will "flee from" us. Like any bully when challenged, the evil one will run away. Will he return? You can count on it. Spiritual warfare will be over only in the life to come, not in this life. We must be ever on guard.

How does the Devil operate? He plays on our pride, particularly wounded pride. He tells us what we want to hear. He whispers in our ear, planting thoughts, suggestions, and ideas in our minds. In the middle of an argument we have all heard his voice—*You don't have to take this kind of stuff. Who do they think they are? Show them who they're trying to push around!* He tells us all the things our pride loves to hear.

The Devil wants to stir up conflicts. He is the author of confusion and discord. He wants to cause disorder, arguments, stress, hurt feelings, disappointment, anger, and

Notes

"Be sober! Be on the alert! Your adversary the Devil is prowling around like a roaring lion, looking for anyone he can devour. Resist him, firm in the faith." 1 Peter 5:8-9

"Let us draw near with a true heart in full assurance of faith." Hebrews 10:22

"But if anyone obeys his word, God's love is truly made complete in him." 1 John 2:5, NIV

disruption. He constantly works to destroy our relationships, especially within the family of faith.

How do we resist the Devil? The same way Jesus did. He not only quoted Scripture but also obeyed it (Matt. 4:1-11). Proverbs 13:10 warns that pride leads to arguments. The next time we get into an argument, that verse can be a vivid reminder to examine the issue of personal pride. We don't have to give in to the Devil if we recognize how he works and are willing to submit to God.

Content Points

1. Living in submission to God gives us strength to withstand Satan's attacks.
2. We must always be on guard for spiritual warfare.
3. Satan plays on our pride to sow discord and disorder and to destroy relationships.

Discussioin Questions

1. Do you think about spiritual warfare as something that affects your everyday life? Why or why not?
2. Read 1 Peter 5:8-9. If we are not aware of our enemy, we will be vulnerable to his attacks. In what ways do we need to "be sober" and "be on the alert" regarding the Devil's attacks?

Application Ideas

1. How do you frequently face temptation ...
    - In the company of specific individuals?
    - In particular locations?
    - Doing particular activities?
    - In physical circumstances such as stress, fatigue, or loneliness?
2. What can you do to avoid those situations? If the situation cannot be avoided, how can you "be on the alert" to defend yourself against temptation and spiritual attack?

[8]Draw near to God, and He will draw near to you. Cleanse your hands, sinners, and purify your hearts, double-minded people!

C. "Draw near to God" (v. 8)—Drawing "near to God" is terminology that describes the special function of priests. However, all believers now are priests (1 Pet. 2:5,9). As incredible as it sounds, God invites each of us to reverently approach Him. When we do, He promises to "draw near" to us. He will not evade us or put us off.

Obviously, to draw near to Him we must first submit ourselves to Him as Lord of our lives and resist the Devil's efforts to lead us away from Him. Assuming we are submitting and resisting, how do we "draw near"? Simply stated, the more time we spend alone with God, the nearer we draw to Him. The more we hear and obey His Word, the nearer we draw to Him. The more we follow His leadership, the closer we can stay to Him.

The nearer we are to God, the better we get along with people. If our attitudes towards Him are right, then our actions towards others probably will be right also. We will never be what God desires unless we spend time with Him. Let us find time, make time, schedule time every day to draw near to the Father. The conflict in our lives might be in direct proportion to the time we spend (or do not spend) with God.

"If you love me, you will obey what I command." John 14:15

"How I love Your teaching! It is my meditation all day long." Psalm 119:97

"If it is possible, as far as it depends on you, live at peace with everyone." Romans 12:18, NIV

Content Points

1. Christians are invited to "draw near" to God, a privilege reserved for priests in the Old Testament. (See Ezek. 40:46; 45:4.)
2. We draw near to God by spending time with Him in His Word, and seeking to follow Him in obedience.
3. If our heart and attitudes are right toward God, they will be right toward others as well. Relational conflict reflects our relationship with God.

Discussioin Questions

1. In addition to spending time in God's Word and seeking to live in obedience to it, what are other ways we can draw near to God?
2. Agree or disagree: Conflict with others is a reflection of our close relationship with God.

Application Ideas

1. Describe your current walk with God.
   - close as inches
   - feet apart
   - distant yards
   - miles away
2. My time with God in prayer and His Word is ...
   - regular
   - occasional
   - nonexistent
3. Do you see a relationship between ideas one and two? If so, what is it?
4. If you desire a more vibrant and consistent prayer life, what steps will you take to draw even closer to God? List one or two in the margin.

Notes

"If we say, 'We have no sin,' we are deceiving ourselves, and the truth is not in us. If we confess our sins, He is faithful and righteous to forgive us our sins and to cleanse us from all unrighteousness." 1 John 1:8-9

*[8]Draw near to God, and He will draw near to you. Cleanse your
hands, sinners, and purify your hearts, double-minded people!
[9]Be miserable and mourn and weep. Your laughter must change to
mourning and your joy to sorrow. [10]Humble yourselves before the
Lord, and He will exalt you.*

D. "Cleanse your hands . . . and purify your hearts" (vv. 8-10)—This admonition is addressed to believers. We are "sinners" and "double-minded people," for on occasion we follow the pull of our sinful human nature rather than the tug of the Spirit; we go our way instead of God's way. Read John 1:8-9 in the margin. The further we get from God, the blinder we are to our sinfulness and our need for forgiveness. When we draw near to God, we increasingly become aware of how far short we fall from His standard of righteousness.

We all, therefore, find that we regularly need to "cleanse" our "hands" and "purify" our "hearts." "Hands" and "hearts" refer to actions and attitudes. How do we clean up our act? First John 1:9 answers that question.

The kind of confession about which John wrote happens, of course, in the spirit of repentance. James 4:9-10 is a strong call to repentance. Repentance—basically a change of mind—results in a change of direction; but sorrow about past sins is part of that process. Regret by itself is not repentance. The road to Christian joy runs through the valley of regret.

When we see our sins from God's perspective, we will indeed "be miserable and mourn and weep." "Miserable" refers to an inner feeling of unhappiness, in this case stemming from an awareness of sin's destructive impact on self, others, and our relationship with God.

"Mourn" refers to passionate grief and sorrow. "Weep" points to the outward display of grief. Obeying these commands means one genuinely repents and mourns sin in a serious manner.

Turning "laughter" and "joy" related to the fleeting pleasures of sinful behavior into "mourning" and "sorrow" indicates a radical change in our point of view. The word translated "sorrow" is composed of the words "down" and "eye." It describes the aching shame that makes the guilty lower their eyes.

This misery, when it signifies genuine repentance, is the necessary doorway to Christian joy. Those who repent and purify their lives will have every reason to laugh and rejoice.

In verse 10 James summed up the path that leads to genuine repentance—"humble yourselves before the Lord." This is the only proper attitude for us sinners, whether we are saved or not. Seldom do we find it easy to admit to God or even to ourselves that we have sinned.

Owning up to our measure of responsibility, such as our fault in a dispute with others, is especially hard for us. Why?

It hurts our pride. We like to feel good about ourselves, so we rationalize our sins and try to hide them from others. When we purposefully draw near to God, we become more aware of His greatness and holiness and of our own smallness and sinfulness. We acknowledge our lives are an open book to Him. So we humble ourselves, confess our sins, and seek His cleansing. When we take these actions, He cleanses us.

God does more than forgive us. He "will exalt" those of us who "humble" ourselves before Him. Perhaps James was remembering Jesus' words in Matthew 23:12. Exalting us, in part, means He returns us to His fellowship and useful service.

Since Jesus said the command to love one another stands alongside the command to love God, our most grievous sins often are committed against people. When our self-centered actions hurt people in some way, let's not minimize what we have done. It may not seem a big deal to us, but it is to them.

Instead, let's make our best effort to resolve the conflict. Let's be willing to apologize for our actions and attitudes, make restitution if appropriate, and ask their forgiveness. This step is so hard that many who would really like to resolve conflicts just aren't willing to pay the price. God paid the supreme price to reconcile us to Himself. With God's gracious help, let us do all we can to seek reconciliation with those who are estranged from us.

Content Points

1. Even though we are Christians, we are still sinners and often fall into sin.
2. Drawing near to God must begin with repentance and confession of sin.
3. Repentance is a process:
   - sorrow for sin
   - a change of mind about the direction we are headed
   - humbling ourselves before God
   - turning around and heading in a different direction
4. If we learn to see sin from God's perspective, we will indeed be broken in repentance.

Discussioin Questions

1. When James addressed "sinners" and "double-minded people," how do we feel when we realize he was talking to Christians?
2. James said we should "Be miserable and mourn and weep." Why should we want to see our "laughter change to mourning and our joy to sorrow"?
3. Why do you think God exalts us when we humble ourselves?

"Whoever exalts himself will be humbled, and whoever humbles himself will be exalted." Matthew 23:12

"And all of you clothe yourselves with humility toward one another, because God resists the proud, but gives grace to the humble. Humble yourselves therefore under the mighty hand of God, so that He may exalt you in due time." 1 Peter 5:5-6

"If I had cherished sin in my heart, the Lord would not have listened; but God has surely listened and heard my voice in prayer. Praise be to God, who has not rejected my prayer or withheld his love from me!" Psalm 66:18-20

"Your iniquities have separated you from your God; your sins have hidden his face from you, so that he will not hear." Isaiah 59:2

Notes

Application Ideas

1. Read Psalm 66:18-20 and Isaiah 59:2 in the margin. Will you make confession of sin a daily part of your prayer life?
2. Confession and repentance are specific actions. When you confess your sin, don't simply say, "forgive me for my sin." Be detailed and specific:
   - Forgive me for my attitude today toward (name).
   - Forgive me for knowingly listening to office gossip.
   - Forgive me for my impatience with the kids at dinner.
3. Part of the process of confession and repentance was described as "turning around and heading in a different direction." As you daily confess your sin, also consider what actions may be necessary to "head in a different direction."

[11]Don't criticize one another, brothers. He who criticizes a brother or judges his brother criticizes the law and judges the law. But if you judge the law, you are not a doer of the law but a judge. [12]There is one lawgiver and judge who is able to save and to destroy. But who are you to judge your neighbor?

E. Let God be the judge (vv. 11-12)—The last action mentioned helps us experience God's guidance in spiritual struggles. We must avoid harsh criticism of fellow believers. Make no mistake, judgmental criticism characterizes the behavior of worldly-minded Christians who lack humility.

The single use of "brothers" and the two uses of "brother" in verse 11 emphasize James was dealing with a matter that threatened church harmony—"don't criticize one another." The Greek construction prohibits action in progress, so James was aware that some in the churches were causing trouble by speaking critically of other members. Sounds contemporary, doesn't it?

The term for "criticize" means literally "speak against." It implies sharp criticism against persons. "Slander" is a possible translation of the word. Speaking against one another is never appropriate. While we can't help forming opinions, we can refrain from criticizing those who disagree with our views.

Speaking against others is a way of condemning them. Such evil speaking includes finding fault with others, putting them down, or gossiping about them. This type of behavior breeds an atmosphere of anger and hostility that results in fights and quarrels that fracture church fellowship.

James identified speaking against a fellow believer with judging that believer. "To judge" means "to pronounce condemnation on someone." The only way we correctly could judge another person would be to know everything about him or her. Judgment thus requires the kind of knowledge only God possesses. How arrogant to think we can know another person's motives or intentions!

One who commits this sin actually "criticizes the law and judges the law." James probably was referring to the royal law—"love your neighbor as yourself" (Jas. 2:8). To speak against a brother or sister is to break that law. Those who deliberately break a law place themselves above the law. They declare in effect, "This bad law is unnecessary and unworthy of our obedience." Those who "judge the law" in this way are no longer doers of the law (1:22). They neither keep it nor submit to it.

James gave another reason we should not criticize and judge each other. The right of judgment belongs to God alone—"There is one lawgiver and judge" (4:12). Since the royal law to love our neighbor originated with God, only He is qualified to determine who has kept it. He alone can correctly judge human character and motives.

Lacking this ability, we do well to assume others are innocent until proven guilty and to speak of them from that viewpoint. Only by doing so can we refrain from damaging reputations and destroying Christian fellowship.

God is the "one who is able to save and to destroy," that is, who has the power to judge. He is Lord of life and death. He has absolute authority to reward those who obey His law and punish those who violate it. His acquittal or conviction is final—and eternal.

James closed this subject with a blunt question—"But who are you who judge your neighbor?" A more literal translation could be: "But you! Who are you? The judger of the neighbor?" These words serve as a pointing finger that singles us out one by one. These words shame us for judging a "neighbor" and stress that we have no rights in this area.

James was not condemning honest discussion or constructive criticism among believers. Nor was he saying we do not need civil courts and judges. He condemned jealous, unkind, and critical attitudes of Christians who are always ready to put others down by finding fault. In one church a lady was spreading rumors about the pastor. On her fifth phone call she was told that her story could not be true.
"Why do you say that?" she replied?

"Because I know our pastor, and he wouldn't do that."

Such criticism would stop in many churches if we were just not gullible enough to believe everything we hear.

"Do not judge, and you will not be judged. Do not condemn, and you will not be condemned. Forgive, and you will be forgiven." Luke 6:37, NIV

Notes

Content Points

1. While we may have differences of perspective or opinion, we should not speak against or condemn our Christian brothers and sisters.
2. To condemn is equivalent to judging, something that only God can do.
3. Only God is qualified to determine who is keeping the law.
4. In judging others, we actually set ourselves up above the law.

Discussioin Questions

1. How good are we at judging human character and motives? When we misjudge someone, what negative effects does it have on our relationship with that person?
2. How often do we jump to conclusions about someone else's actions or motives? Do we need to "assume innocence until proven guilty"?

Application Ideas

1. Do you ever find yourself engaged in fault-finding? Do you sometimes have an unkind, critical attitude toward others? If so, ask God's forgiveness. Give the right to judge others back to Him.
2. Do you ever say or hear someone say, "He thinks such and such" or "She just wants to ..."? How do we know what people are thinking and intending? How do we know their motives? What will you do to be more self-conscious about this form of judging?

[13]Come now, you who say, "Today or tomorrow we will travel to such and such a city and spend a year there and do business and make a profit." [14]You don't even know what tomorrow will bring—what your life will be! For you are a bit of smoke that appears for a little while, then vanishes. [15]Instead, you should say, "If the Lord wills, we will live and do this or that." [16]But as it is, you boast in your arrogance. All such boasting is evil. [17]So, for the person who knows to do good and doesn't do it, it is a sin.

III. *Emphasize God's Will* (4:13-17)

Christians often talk about wanting to know the will of God for their lives. For many of us a better question is this: *Am I willing and ready to do the will of God as He reveals it to me?* We fear the unknown, so to write God a blank check, so to speak, can scare us. It would be safer to plan our lives for ourselves, except for one thing: God's will for us. While costly, God's will is always best for us. He loves us, and we are foolish indeed not to trust His love. Verses 13-17 point out three mistakes people make regarding the future.

A. Acknowledge the uncertainty of life (vv. 13-14)—Verse 13 begins with "Come now," an invitation to reflect on the importance of following God's will. Life is uncertain, brief, and unpredictable. We routinely presume on tomorrow as we plan our finances and our schedules. So did all the people who died today in accidents. We dare not take tomorrow for granted.

Verse 13 paints a word picture of a business meeting among a group of merchants making confident plans for the future. We can imagine them deliberating over the location, the starting date, the duration, and the anticipated profits of a projected financial venture. The last three uses of 'and" in their conversation suggest confident and animated strategizing. Aside from the fact that "do business" also can be translated "to exploit" (see 2 Pet. 2:3), what did James see wrong in this meeting? Verse 14 tells us.

Those making business plans gave no thought to the uncertainty of life. "You do not know what your life will be like tomorrow." He could have added "much less a year from now." James perhaps had Proverbs 27:1 in mind here. Boasting about tomorrow is a presumption, "for you do not know what a day might bring forth."

The translation of "what your life will be" (Jas. 4:14) also can be translated as an independent question—"What is your life?" James's meaning is clear either way. Every human life is "a bit of smoke that appears for a little while, then vanishes." The Greek word for "smoke" also can mean "vapor," both of which dissipate in a short while. All human life is transitory and sooner or later will end in death. Refusing to see that truth is mystifying self-deception. Not applying it to daily living is blatant arrogance!

Don't hear these words of James say making long-range plans is a bad idea. On the contrary, Luke 14:28 affirms that planning is a wise endeavor. Scripture teaches us to be prudent and to be good stewards in all areas of life. All of our planning needs to take into account the plain fact that we have little and often no control over the way events unfold. Anything can happen to any of us at any moment. Only our loving Father in heaven knows what lies in store for us, so the wisest and most prudent element in any planning is to seek His guidance and to do His will.

"Don't boast about tomorrow, for you don't know what a day might bring." Proverbs 27:1

"Then I'll say to myself, 'You have many goods stored up for many years. Take it easy; eat, drink, and enjoy yourself.' But God said to him, 'You fool! This very night your life is demanded of you. And the things you have prepared—whose will they be?'" Luke 12:19-20

Content Points

1. Life is uncertain, and we cannot take tomorrow for granted.
2. We need to live in the reality that life is transitory.
3. All planning should be done in light of seeking to follow God's will and wisdom.

Notes

"Let him who boasts boast in the Lord."
1 Corinthians 1:31

Discussioin Questions

1. What are some ways that we routinely take tomorrow for granted?
2. When we live with a transitory view of life, how will it affect our planning and decisions?
3. How would planning our lives in light of God's leadership change our priorities and thinking?

Application Ideas

What are your long-range plans and goals? Are these your plans or God's plans? If you truly plan on following God's Word and His guidance, what do you need to do (or not do) in order for that to happen?

[15]Instead, you should say, "If the Lord wills, we will live and do this or that." [16]But as it is, you boast in your arrogance. All such boasting is evil.

B. Include God in all planning (vv. 15-16)—Since the future is unknown and since life is short and uncertain, we need always to acknowledge that God is in control. Remembering that He is our loving Father in heaven, let's readily confess our dependence on Him, not only in making and carrying out our plans but also in every area of life.

Rather than presumptuously making decisions about what we will do or plan to achieve, we need to remind ourselves "if the Lord wills, we will live and do this or that." This does not mean we simply are to tack on the words "if the Lord wills" at the end of our planning. This qualifying clause is to be more than a mechanical, meaningless, thoughtless repetition of pious words. It is to express our recognition of God's supremacy. He is in control of life, so let us submit to Him in humility and dependence. People can make plans for the future, but God must be a part of that process.

Verse 16 addresses believers who presumptuously plan and act independently of God—"You boast in your arrogance." "Arrogance" means "to glorify oneself." We easily kid ourselves by thinking we are self-made people. "All such boasting is evil." Let's guard against thinking our talents, environment, and opportunities originated with us. We stray far from the truth when we glorify ourselves and forget God. Boasting is most appropriate and commendable when it glorifies God (1 Cor. 1:31).

Content Points

1. God is in control of all things.
2. Our plans are only valid to the extent that God allows them to take place.
3. Making plans without seeking God's leadership is like "boasting," as if we are the ones in control.

Discussioin Questions

1. How can making plans for the future be "boasting" and "arrogant"?
2. In light of what James said, how should we go about making plans?
3. How do we make wise, long-range plans that are not just our own but include God's counsel?

Application Ideas

1. What plans do you have for each of the following areas? What role has God played in your plans?
   - employment
   - for your home, family
   - savings, retirement, and travel
2. If your plans don't work out the way you want, are you prepared to follow God's leadership wherever it takes you? to view God's plan as "Plan A"?
3. How can plans include service to God in our churches and communities? Consider ministries to those in need, to others who are ill, and to the unsaved all around us.

[17]*So, for the person who knows to do good and doesn't do it, it is a sin.*

C. Do good (v. 17)—This verse warns us about the sin of procrastination. James indicated that putting off doing the right thing leads to sins of omission. Most of us know the right thing to do, but that doesn't mean we will do it. Not doing what we know to be right is just as wrong as doing what we know to be sinful.

Although the words of this independent saying or proverb relate specifically to the immediate context, they have a wider, more general application to the Christian life. "The person who knows" carries the implication of having been fully warned. The context (Jas. 4:13-16) emphasizes that God controls the future of each individual. Thus we need to depend on Him as we plan, work, and fulfill all responsibilities day by day. Knowing this, we are foolish indeed to ignore God and continue to go our own way with self-assured pride.

When we know what should be done and fail to do it, our omission is sin. Knowing what is right obligates us to do it. Failing to do good when we have the opportunity to do so is sin. Sins of omission are as much disobedience to God as sins of commission.

Jesus' most serious words of condemnation are aimed at sins of omission (Matt. 25:31-46). The emphasis in James is on *doing* God's will, not just on knowing it. Believers' last earthly claim must not be that they knew the right thing to do but just didn't get around to it.

Notes

James illustrated the behavior of people who fail to submit to the Lord and explained such as presumption against God. This manner of behavior ignores His will. Unless we submit humbly to God, we will presume on Him and fail to do His will. His will always is for us to seek what is best for others rather than for ourselves.

Content Points

1. Not doing what we know to be the right thing is just as much sin as doing what we know is wrong.
2. Sins of omission are as much disobedience to God as sins of commission.
3. In the context of this passage, knowing that God holds the future yet not seeking His leadership in our future, is sin.

Discussioin Questions

1. What are some of our common sins of omission?
2. How do we justify our sins of omission?
3. How does observing the life of Jesus through His Word help us identify sins of omission?

Application Ideas

1. What is something you know you should be doing but you are not being obedient in that way?
2. Who is someone you should be helping?
3. How do you try to justify or rationalize your lack of action?
4. Based on James 4:17, what are you going to do now?

SUMMARY

1. The cravings to possess, for self-sufficiency, and for the world's friendship bring us into conflict with others.

2. We must first be submitted to God's lordship and leadership in our lives to be able to resist the Devil's attacks.

3. In submitting and humbling ourselves to God with clean hands and a pure heart, we must repent and confess our sins.

4. To criticize and judge others correctly requires the kind of knowledge that only God possesses. Only God has the right to judge. Our judgment is self-righteous and brings disruption to our fellowship.

5. All plans for the future should be made with the acknowledgment that God is in control, not us. To plan otherwise is arrogant and presumptuous.

[2]You desire and do not have. You murder and covet and cannot obtain. You fight and war. You do not have because you do not ask. [3]You ask and don't receive because you ask wrongly, so that you may spend it on your desires for pleasure.

God wants us to be asking children. He has limitless love, overflowing grace, unending mercy, and great wisdom—all of which are available to His children. Yet He does not always respond the way we expect when we ask. James pointed out that we might not receive an answer because we are not asking with the right motives or purposes. So then, how should we ask?

1. We should ask in faith, trusting God is able to do "above and beyond all that we ask or think" (Eph. 3:20).

2. We should ask with clean hearts. Until we repent of known sin in our lives, our prayers are little more than an empty religious activity. "Your iniquities have built barriers between you and your God, and your sins have made Him hide His face from you so that He does not listen" (Isa. 59:2).

3. We should ask in accord with God's revealed purposes in the world—"Your will be done" (Matt. 6:10; see also 1 John 5:14-15). God may say no because our requests may not be consistent with His purposes or because the timing is not according to His schedule. Because His ways are not our ways, we may not fully understand His answer.

4. We can ask trusting that God's wisdom is infinitely greater than our human wisdom (Job 28:12-28; Isa. 55:8-9). He sees the end from the beginning, so He knows all that will happen as a result of His response to our requests. Because God's vision is greater than our limited views of life, He knows what is best for us in the long run; therefore, He may not grant our requests in ways we expect or want.

5. In making our requests, we can trust God's love for us (John 3:16). We can trust that how and when God's answers, He is acting in our overall best interests because He loves us.

1. Mark Buchanan. *The Rest of God* (Nashville: W Publishing Group, 2006), 121.
2. *The Baptist Hymnal* (Nashville: Convention Press, 1991), 329.

JAMES 5:1-12 (HCSB)

1 Come now, you rich people! Weep and wail over the miseries
that are coming on you. 2 Your wealth is ruined: your clothes
are moth-eaten; 3 your silver and gold are corroded, and their
corrosion will be a witness against you and will eat your flesh
like fire. You stored up treasure in the last days! 4 Look! The pay
that you withheld from the workers who reaped your fields cries
out, and the outcry of the harvesters has reached the ears of the
Lord of Hosts. 5 You have lived luxuriously on the land and have
indulged yourselves. You have fattened your hearts for the day
of slaughter. 6 You have condemned—you have murdered—the
righteous man; he does not resist you.

7 Therefore, brothers, be patient until the Lord's coming. See
how the farmer waits for the precious fruit of the earth and is
patient with it until it receives the early and the late rains. 8 You
also must be patient. Strengthen your hearts, because the Lord's
coming is near.

9 Brothers, do not complain about one another, so that you
will not be judged. Look, the judge stands at the door!

10 Brothers, take the prophets who spoke in the Lord's name as
an example of suffering and patience. 11 See, we count as blessed
those who have endured. You have heard of Job's endurance and
have seen the outcome from the Lord: the Lord is very compas-
sionate and merciful.

12 Now above all, my brothers, do not swear, either by heaven
or by earth or with any other oath. Your "yes" must be "yes," and
your "no" must be "no," so that you won't fall under judgment.

Unit Four: Trust God!

Lesson Seven

ENDURE PATIENTLY (JAMES 5:1-12)

I. **Endure Patiently Even Though Some Misuse Wealth (5:1-6)**

   A. The Accumulation of Wealth (vv. 2-3)

   B. The Appropriation of Wealth (v. 4)

   C. The Allocation of Wealth (v. 5)

   D. The Application of Wealth (v. 6)

II. **Endure Patiently Because of the Lord's Coming (5:7-9)**

III. **Endure Patiently Following Old Testament Examples (5:10-11)**

IV. **Endure Patiently as You Speak (5:12)**

LEARNING GOALS

As a result of studying this session, learners will:

- *Explain the difference in tone between 5:1-6 and 5:7-12*
- *Identify four ways wealth is commonly abused*
- *Describe why and how believers can strengthen their hearts to endure whatever comes*
- *State the benefits we share with those who have set the example of endurance*
- *Cite the priority and importance of consistently speaking truth*

Notes

Chapter four ends with a denunciation of wealthy and arrogant merchants who plan profitable enterprises without any thought of God and His will. Chapter five begins in a similar vein with the target being rich landowners who apparently were unbelievers. James's words to them are the harshest denunciations in the letter.

The chapter ends, however, with words of comfort and guidance for those being victimized by the wealthy. So James 5:1-6 and 5:7-12 address two different groups respectively, which accounts for the contrast between the two passages.

1Come now, you rich people! Weep and wail over the miseries that
are coming on you. 2Your wealth is ruined: your clothes are moth-
eaten; 3your silver and gold are corroded, and their corrosion will
be a witness against you and will eat your flesh like fire. You stored
up treasure in the last days! 4Look! The pay that you withheld from
the workers who reaped your fields cries out, and the outcry of the
harvesters has reached the ears of the Lord of Hosts. 5You have lived
luxuriously on the land and have indulged yourselves. You have fat-
tened your hearts for the day of slaughter. 6You have condemned—
you have murdered—the righteous man; he does not resist you.

I. *Endure Patiently Although Some Misuse Wealth* (vv. 1-6)

Scripture nowhere teaches that being wealthy is evil; however, it does teach that being wealthy is dangerous. Wealth brings with it a false sense of security and importance. It fosters a powerful desire to control others and to get richer and richer by any means. Through the years the wealthy far more often than not have exploited the poor to increase their wealth. James warned that a time of reckoning would come for those who exploit others.

"Come now, you rich people!" (v. 1) is an invitation for self-centered rich people to hear James's message of God's judgment on them. "You rich people" is literally "the rich," indicating James addressed them as a class. James was aware of righteous and upstanding wealthy people, but they were exceptions to the rule. The people who had chosen as their first love wealth over God faced divine judgment.

James exhorted the rich to cry aloud in anguish for God's judgment that was coming on them. He described this judgment as "miseries." We know that throughout the Bible God's messages of judgment were designed to lead sinners to repentance (Ezek. 33:11; 2 Pet. 3:9), so we may assume this was part of James's purpose. Certainly he also wanted to reassure suffering Christians that God indeed would judge those who oppressed them.

"For the love of money is a root of all kinds of evil, and by craving it, some have wandered away from the faith and pierced themselves with many pains." 1 Timothy 6:10

"Again I tell you, it is easier for a camel to go through the eye of a needle than for a rich person to enter the kingdom of God." Matthew 19:24

"You say, 'I am rich; I have acquired wealth and do not need a thing.' But you do not realize that you are wretched, pitiful, poor, blind and naked." Revelation 3:17, NIV

"Give me neither poverty nor riches, but give me only my daily bread." Proverbs 30:8b, NIV

Perhaps James also was warning believers not to follow the wealthy people's example of wrongfully gaining and using wealth. We need to take that particular message to heart. Few aspects of contemporary life are as potentially dangerous to our spiritual health as our attitude toward money and the things it can buy. If we are to endure worldly pressures and remain faithful to the Lord, we must avoid four common abuses of wealth. Wealth can be abused by accumulation, appropriation, allocation, and application.

Content Points

1. Wealth is not evil, but it is dangerous.
2. Wealthy persons who cheat and oppress the poor will receive God's judgment.

Discussion Questions

1. What are the dangers of wealth?
2. How does the materialistic focus of our society make it hard to keep our priorities straight regarding money?

Application Ideas

1. What "things" are on your personal wish list? What does that list reflect about your personal priorities?
2. After essential bills (housing, utilities, transportation), how much do you spend on yourself? How much do you spend on others? How much do you give away?
3. How much do you pay in a year on credit card interest? How much do you give in a year to your church? Is there anything askew between those figures?

2Your wealth is ruined: your clothes are moth-eaten; 3your silver and gold are corroded, and their corrosion will be a witness against you and will eat your flesh like fire. You stored up treasure in the last days!

A. The accumulation of wealth (vv. 2-3)—We can abuse accumulation of wealth (vv. 2-3). God allows us to make money so we can pay our own way through life and can help others, but He never intends for us to be greedy hoarders. Verses 2-3 are not a rebuke of saving, which obviously is a vital component of stewardship.

These verses refer to getting more and more simply for the sake of getting more and more. Greed tends to grow in proportion to accumulated wealth. In an age characterized by growing affluence, how desperately we need to guard against becoming obsessed with obtaining wealth!

Selfishly gathered and guarded possessions never last. James declared that hoarded "wealth is ruined." Probably he had in mind storing such produce as corn and grain until it rotted. What a waste when so many were hungry! The

"Don't collect for yourselves treasures on earth, where moth and rust destroy and where thieves break in and steal. But collect for yourselves treasures in heaven, where neither moth nor rust destroys, and where thieves don't break in and steal. For where your treasure is, there your heart will be also." Matthew 6:19-21

owners were willing to let their surplus food decay rather than give it to hungry people.

"Clothing" was another form of wealth in that era (v. 2). Paul also referred to this when he declared he had "not coveted anyone's silver or gold or clothing" (Acts 20:33). James reminded these rich folk that their "clothes are moth-eaten." Often moths silently took away the value of the fine garments in storage.

These rich people were deceiving themselves concerning the mass of coins they had saved. They had hoarded "silver and gold" when they could have put it to practical use in helping others (Jas. 5:3). James likely was speaking figuratively when he referred to the coins that "have corroded."

"Corroded" is an intensive verb that means "rusted all the way to the bottom." Of course silver may corrode and gold may tarnish, but neither is likely to rust. James may have meant that wealth becomes worthless when hoarded and not used for good purposes.

Then James personified "corrosion," referring to it as though it could speak and eat. He warned it "will be a witness against" the greedy wealthy people at their judgment. The future tense "will be" may be a hint that they could still change their ways. Apart from repentance, corrosion would "eat [their] flesh like fire" at the time of judgment.

James then underscored a bitter irony—the wealthy were hoarding their goods "in the last days." The "last days" refer to the future judgment. Instead of preparing for the approaching judgment, the greedy rich were focused on hoarding more wealth for their later years. In the long run, being obsessed with gaining wealth leads to eternal loss. It will all be for nothing.

Content Points

1. God intends two primary uses of money: covering personal needs and helping others.
2. We are not to be greedy hoarders, but generous givers.
3. We should be preparing for eternity, not storing up what we cannot keep on earth.

Discussion Questions

1. How much is enough? When does our spending become self-indulgent?
2. What are some ways we trust in money instead of God?

Application Ideas

1. Do you have a long-range financial plan? Does it have a limit on how much you desire to gain and save?
2. Do you have a systematic plan for giving? to your church? to other charities? to people in need?

[4]*Look! The pay that you withheld from the workers who reaped your fields cries out, and the outcry of the harvesters has reached the ears of the Lord of Hosts.*

B. The appropriation of wealth (v. 4)—The appropriation of wealth (v. 4) affords a second possible abuse. God is not only concerned with what we have but also how we got it. There are numerous ways to increase wealth dishonestly. James cited not paying for work done.

"The pay … withheld from the workers who reaped your fields" was marginal to begin with, and these landowners at times refused to pay even that. The word for "fields" is used for estate-like farms, which underlines the wealth of the greedy owners.

Laborers in the first century usually were hired at the beginning of the day for a day's work. Mosaic law commanded that they be paid when the workday was over (Deut. 24:14-15). The reason was clear—those laborers were poor and needy. Food for the day had to be bought with money earned that day.

Workers had no labor unions and few laws to protect them. A person could work all day and the boss could say, "I don't like your work" and refuse to pay. Some might call that "cutting down on expenses," but God calls it stealing.

Unfair treatment of workers is not at all uncommon today. News reports constantly cite situations in which overtime pay was withheld or promised benefits not granted. As companies "downsize" to reduce expenses and pad the bottom line, many employees find their work-loads increasing with no additional compensation.

Corporate fraud has cheated employees of promised pensions and investors of both profits and capital. Although much of this corruption is never reported, we can be sure the Lord is aware of it.

Personifying the fraudulently withheld pay, James declared it constantly "cries out" against the dishonest landowners. That and the "outcry of the harvesters has reached the ears of the Lord of Hosts." This title is an important Old Testament name for God. "Hosts" means "armies," so the title is sometimes translated as "the Lord Almighty."

God still hears the cries of defrauded people. The people who wrongly appropriate their money will answer to Him. We can endure patiently inequities beyond our control, knowing that ultimately God's justice will be served.

In our day, this message about defrauding others cuts both ways—many workers defraud their employers. Some companies factor into their pricing the cost of anticipated thefts by employees. Many workers abuse their office internet access by making purchases, buying merchandise, and exchanging personal e-mails. Others take longer breaks

Do not oppress a hired hand who is poor and needy … You are to pay him his wages each day before the sun sets, because he is poor and depends on them. Otherwise he will cry out to the LORD against you, and you will be held guilty." Deuteronomy 24:14-15

Notes

"Zacchaeus stood up and said to the Lord, 'Look, Lord! Here and now I give half of my possessions to the poor, and if I have cheated anybody out of anything, I will pay back four times the amount.' Jesus said to him, 'Today salvation has come to this house.'"
Luke 19:8-9, NIV

We make a living by what we get;
we make a life by what we give.
—Winston Churchill

than policy allows. All such behavior violates the principle of giving an honest day's labor for a day's pay. Let's keep in mind that God condemns all forms of making money by taking unfair advantage of others.

Content Points

1. God is concerned not only with what we have, but how we got it.
2. We are not to cheat, deceive or otherwise make money through dishonest means or at the expense of others.
3. Employees owe employers an honest day's work, just as the employer owes the employee an honest day's pay.

Discussion Questions

1. What are some ways that many people today make dishonest gain?
2. How does cheating our employer hurt our Christian witness at work?

Application Ideas

1. Do you "cheat" your employer? Are there things you need to do or not do to give a more honest day's work?
2. Read Luke 19:8-9 in the margin. In light of Zacchaeus's actions, what might God be calling you to do about any form of cheating?
3. If you are unclear about what might be considered cheating in your business or hobby, ask the advice of an older person who has shown himself/herself to be an exemplary employee or acqaintance.

[5]You have lived luxuriously on the land and have indulged yourselves. You have fattened your hearts for the day of slaughter.

C. The allocation of wealth (v. 5)—The allocation of wealth is another way it can be abused. God is concerned not only with how we make money but also with how we spend it. As our income grows, the temptation to spend it only on ourselves must be avoided. The more money we make, the easier we can take our cues from the world about how to use it.

Our culture is constantly reinforcing the necessity of spending to bring personal pleasure. We are invited to buy into the philosophy that says, "I'm worth it; I can afford it, so why not?" Just because we can afford something does not mean buying it is a good idea. (See **"Going Deeper—Financial Responsibility,"** p. 144.)

James accused the rich of living "luxuriously on the land" and of having "indulged" themselves." The two Greek verbs for "lived luxuriously" and "have indulged yourselves" are virtual synonyms. The self-indulgent life stood out as a stark contrast to the generally impoverished condition of laborers.

This first verb suggests the practice of sensual self-indulgence, and the second goes much further into sensual darkness—a life immersed in immorality and dissipation. The tense of both verbs suggests such revelry was habitual.

These words portray people in a financial position to do whatever they feel like doing, acting without constraint. Adding "on the land" can mean "on the earth" and may have been a way of indicating that when the earth was gone, these people would have nothing at all.

The complacent rich reminded James of cattle fattening themselves contentedly, not knowing they were readying themselves for "the day of slaughter." To refer to fattening their "hearts" was not unusual. Ancient thought connected the stomach and the heart. The heart was viewed as the seat of both appetites and passions. People who deprive others and pamper themselves in luxury are similar to cattle being fattened in preparation for the slaughter house.

Many of us who never would cheat anyone out of a dime are abusing money in the ways we spend it. What does your checkbook say about your philosophy of spending money? Take time to calculate what percentage of your income in the past month or year was given to advance the Lord's work through your church. Then figure the percentage you spent or gave away to help others.

What implications can you draw from these financial facts? Compare them with the ones below:[1]

- The average donation by adults who attend U.S. Protestant churches is about $17 a week.
- Thirty-three percent of U.S. born-again Christians say it is impossible for them to get ahead in life because of the financial debt they have incurred.
- Statistics from the Internal Revenue Service show that persons whose annual income is less than $25,000 give almost 4 times as much to charity as persons with an income between a half million to a million dollars (based on a percentage of income).

Do you think God is pleased with your priorities? Is your standard of living reasonable? Wrestling with these questions—though not easy—might point to an area in which you need to grow spiritually.

When John Wesley first became a Christian, he had a salary of 30 pounds per year. He lived on 28 pounds, and gave two to the church. When Wesley's salary was increased to 50 pounds per year, he lived on 28, and gave 22 to the church. When Wesley's salary was increased to 100 pounds per year, he lived on 28 and gave 72 to the church.[3] What compassion he must have had for the poor and what trust he must have had in his Heavenly Father.

My experience has been that if you don't start giving away your money when you have very little, you won't do it when you get a lot.
—Robert Bainum[2]

Notes

"So don't worry, saying, 'What will we eat?' or 'What will we drink?' or 'What will we wear?' For Gentiles eagerly seek all these things, and your heavenly Father knows that you need them. But seek first the kingdom of God and His righteousness, and all these things will be provided for you."
Matthew 6:31-33

Content Points

1. God is not only concerned with how we make money, but also with how we spend it.
2. The more money we make, the easier it is to become self-indulgent in how we spend it.
3. The way we spend money betrays the true priorities and values we hold in our hearts.

Discussion Questions

1. What is the difference between "needs" and "wants"? What might we take for granted as "needs" that are actually "wants"?
2. How do television commercials and other advertising convince us that our "wants" are really "needs"?

Application Ideas

1. Have you ever noticed how everyone who drinks beer in television commercials is:
    - having lots of fun
    - surrounded by friends
    - surrounded by the opposite sex
2. Have you ever noticed how the newest electronics are portrayed as:
    - making your life more enjoyable
    - making your life easier
    - rendering your current gadgets obsolete
3. Have you noticed how getting a certain car or truck is portrayed as:
    - giving you freedom
    - making you "hip"
    - getting the girl
    - helping you conquer life's demands (i.e. traffic, kids, schedules)
4. Do you ever find yourself believing ads? (If only I had that, then I ___________.) How much truth is there in these claims?
5. Consider the ways you spend and what you spend it on. How much money do you spend in a month that is not really necessary? What might you do with some of that money that would help others and honor God?

[6]You have condemned—you have murdered—the righteous man; he does not resist you.

D. The application of wealth (v. 6)—The application of wealth, in the sense of how we use the power and influence that comes with it, presents a fourth way to abuse wealth. Wealth brings more than simply the ability to buy what we desire. It gives us influence with others and sometimes places us in authority over them.

James accused the wealthy of grossly misusing their power: "You have condemned—you have murdered—the righteous man; he does not resist you." What "righteous man" did James have in mind? The context commends the view that James was referring to poor people whom the rich people had pushed deep into deadly poverty.

Being in favor with the political and judicial authorities, these rich people thought they could get away with unjustly refusing to pay wages. "The righteous" can refer to all the poor as a class. The last statement in verse 6 thus means, "he [the poor righteous one] does not resist you." Poor people realize the futility of resisting wealthy folk who can pay off the authorities or pay for an army of lawyers to contest any claims against them.

Today some still use money to manipulate and take advantage of others. In some families one person tries to control relatives by threatening to cut them out of the will. In some businesses a manager uses the power to recommend salary increases as a tool to pressure employees into unethical or even immoral acts.

Some interest groups have offered support for certain politicians who agree to work for laws that give their businesses economic advantages over competitors. These are wrong applications of wealth's influence.

Many Christians recognize the influence of money. Wealth has great power. Let us not abuse it but use it in ways that build God's kingdom. Recognize that hoarded wealth will decay and devalue. Those who love money, who are callous or dishonest in gaining it, who use it selfishly, and who abuse its power will give account to Almighty God.

Content Points

1. Wealth brings with it influence and authority.
2. The rich can be tempted to use their power to oppress the poor and powerless in order to make even more money.
3. Christians must avoid the temptation to use the influence of money to manipulate others.
4. The rich will have to give an account before God.

Discussion Questions

1. What are some ways today that people use the power of money to manipulate others?
2. How should we respond to those who might try to manipulate us through the influence of money?

Notes

"Now you can have sincere love for each other as brothers and sisters because you were cleansed from your sins when you accepted the truth of the Good News. So see to it that you really do love each other intensely with all your hearts." 1 Peter 1:22, NLT

"Friends, do not avenge yourselves; instead, leave room for His wrath. For it is written: Vengeance belongs to Me; I will repay, says the Lord." Romans 12:19

Application Ideas

1. Have you ever had an employer seek to influence or even manipulate you to do something you shouldn't do? How did you respond?
2. One of the best ways to defeat temptation is to plan ahead for how to respond to it before it happens. Think about how you would respond to pressure at work to do something unethical.
    - Would you try to skirt the issue?
    - Would you "play along" and try to get out of it without being noticed?
    - Would you stand up to your boss and refuse to do it?
    - Would you quit?

Thinking things through before you are under the pressure of the moment helps you decide how to best respond if the occasion ever arises.

[7]Therefore, brothers, be patient until the Lord's coming. See how the
farmer waits for the precious fruit of the earth and is patient with
it until it receives the early and the late rains. [8]You also must be
patient. Strengthen your hearts, because the Lord's coming is near.
[9]Brothers, do not complain about one another, so that you will not
be judged. Look, the judge stands at the door!

II. Endure Patiently Because of the Lord's Coming (vv. 7-9)

In verses 1-6 James exposed and condemned the actions of the rich who were guilty of exploiting others. Beginning in verse 7 he addressed the victims of exploitation and exhorted them to hold fast to their faith. The remainder of the letter is remarkably tender. The word for "brothers" occurs five times in the last 14 verses, and references to the closeness of Christian fellowship (such as "one another" and "among you") add a warmth to this passage.

"Therefore" (Jas. 5:7) points back to the promise that "the Lord of Hosts" (v. 4) would deal properly with abusive wealthy people. Based on that truth, James exhorted believers to "be patient, brethren, until the Lord's coming." The word for "patient," used twice in this verse, means "long-suffering." It suggests self-restraint, not trying to get even for a wrong that has been done. In this context the word has the added sense of expectant waiting.

James could not say, of course, how soon Jesus' triumphant return would take place. The word for "coming" depicts a king's visit to one of his cities. (See **"Going Deeper—New Testament Terms for Christ's Second**

Coming," p. 144.) How different this second coming of Christ will be from the first!

Three times verses 7-9 refer to the glorious truth that the Lord Jesus is coming back. That is the ultimate assurance that God is in control of our world, even when the world seems to be out of control.

History is moving toward an honorable and victorious climax. God is in control of history because it really is "His story." He has it all planned out; everything is on schedule; nothing is late; it's all moving to His perfect cadence.

James instructed his readers to be patient in this sin-cursed world just as "the farmer" is patient while waiting "for the precious fruit of the earth." The crop is "precious" (valuable) because the farmer and his family depend on it for survival. They have absolutely no control, however, over many factors that affect it—wind, rain, market prices, availability and quality of labor, and so forth. They have to wait "for the early and late [autumn and spring] rains."

Farmers need both rainy seasons to produce a successful harvest. They also wait a long time for the crops to mature. This requires patience. They can do nothing to bring the rain or speed up the growth of the plants.

Though patient, farmers are not idle. They are busy all year long—repairing or maintaining tools and machinery, preparing the soil, sowing the seed, fertilizing, weeding, and keeping animals away from the crops. While they cannot control the end result, they keep busy with what they can control. Likewise, we don't know and cannot control when Jesus will return, but we know what to do until that time. He has given us the Great Commission; and while we anticipate His coming, we have plenty to keep us busy.

Therefore James used the illustration of the farmer to encourage believers then and now to "be patient" as we endure this world's injustices (v. 8). He tells us to "strengthen [our] hearts." We need inner courage and strength to face difficulties without sinking into bitterness or despair. How do we strengthen our hearts? Hebrews says we do so by "keeping our eyes on Jesus" (read Heb. 12:1-12).

"Let us fix our eyes on Jesus, the author and perfecter of our faith ... Consider him who endured such opposition from sinful men, so that you will not grow weary and lose heart."
Hebrews 12:2,3, NIV

James gave a reason to be patient and to strengthen our hearts—"the Lord's coming is near." We are not to be concerned about the number of years between Christ's first and second comings. Rather, we are to focus on how we should cope with circumstances in light of His return. When we look at time from God's point of view—that of eternity—Jesus' return is always near (see 2 Pet. 3:8). This truth gives us confidence as we wait for Him. God is not ignoring the wicked; in God's timing, they certainly will face judgment for their deeds.

Verse 9 repeats the affectionate address "brothers," but then warns them to act like brothers. Evidently they were

Notes

"Do everything without complaining or arguing." Philippians 2:14, NIV

"Do not judge, so that you won't be judged. For with the judgment you use, you will be judged, and with the measure you use, it will be measured to you. Why do you look at the speck in your brother's eye, but don't notice the log in your own eye?" Matthew 7:1-3

complaining "about one another," since he commanded them to stop this practice. "Complain" literally means "to groan or to sigh heavily." This refers to an inner distress of bitterness or resentment.

Do you often find yourself complaining about other folk? Some people constantly complain. A complaining spirit takes offence at any little thing. Some have a sour disposition, find fault with everyone, and are angry when others are more prosperous, honored, and appreciated than themselves. They seem to feel they have a right and duty to complain if everything is not done precisely as they think it should be.

This complaining attitude is rooted in pride and is completely contrary to the gospel. If we are prone to find fault with people and to shine the spotlight of attention on the fault, we simply need to repent. Ask God to teach us to be loving brothers and sisters to fellow believers.

Continuing to complain about others will result in judgment. James emphasized the certainty, suddenness, and nearness of judgment. Complainers will be "judged" for their attitudes if they do not change. Already in 4:11-12 James had warned against judging others.

Complaining against fellow believers is the same as judging them. If the criticism is vocal, we have seriously misused the tongue (see 3:1-12). Besides, such judging usurps the power of the real "Judge." That genuine Judge, by the way, "stands at the door." While this phrase could mean He is close enough to hear every complaint believers make about one another, it reminds us that the coming of the Lord is near. The promise of His return is both a consolation and warning.

Content Points

1. We should endure mistreatment patiently, knowing that God will judge those who mistreat us.
2. God is in control of all history, and Jesus will return at the appointed time.
3. We shouldn't focus on timetables but on how to cope with life's circumstances until Jesus returns.
4. While we can't know or control when Christ will return, we have plenty of His work to do in the meantime.
5. Complaining about others is a form of judging them. If we do so, we will be the ones judged when Christ returns.

Discussion Questions

1. When others wrong us, why do we find it hard not to get even? Why is it hard to leave justice to God?
2. As Christians, we say we believe that God is in control. What are some of the things we think, say, and do that show we often don't really believe that?
3. What does God want us to be doing until Christ returns?
4. Why is complaining about others contrary to the gospel?

Application Ideas

1. Is there someone in your life with whom you really want to "get even"?
   - Read Romans 12:19 in your Bible. What do you need to do?
   - Now read Luke 6:27-28 in the margin. What specific ways can you demonstrate to those who mistreat you that will apply what Jesus taught in this passage?
2. Do you find yourself frequently complaining about others at home? at work? at church? Do you see how your complaints are a form of judgment? Are you willing to let God do the judging?

"But I say to you who listen: Love your enemies, do good to those who hate you, bless those who curse you, pray for those who mistreat you."
Luke 6:27-28

10 Brothers, take the prophets who spoke in the Lord's name as an example of suffering and patience. 11 See, we count as blessed those who have endured. You have heard of Job's endurance and have seen the outcome from the Lord: the Lord is very compassionate and merciful.

III. *Endure Patiently Following Old Testament Examples* (vv. 10-11)

In verse 10 James used "the prophets who spoke in the Lord's name as an example of "suffering and patience." They communicated God's word, serving as His instruments and representatives. As a result of faithful service to God, the prophets often were persecuted.

James did not identify by name any particular prophet, but the Old Testament noted the mistreatment of many of God's messengers. Despite their suffering, the prophets responded with long-suffering patience and expectation of God's intervention. For this reason the prophets are an example to believers, a model or pattern we can imitate in times of trial and mistreatment.

"So Pashhur had Jeremiah the prophet beaten and put him in the stocks."
Jeremiah 20:2

"Then the priests and prophets said to the officials and all the people, 'This man deserves the death sentence because he has prophesied against this city, as you have heard with your own ears.'" Jeremiah 26:11

What will be the result of our endurance? The short answer is that we will be blessed—"See, we count as blessed those who have endured" (v. 11). James gave a longer answer earlier in his letter—"the testing of your faith produces endurance. But endurance must do its complete work, so that you may be mature and complete, lacking nothing. … Blessed is a man who endures trials, because when he asses the test he will receive the crown of life that He has promised to those who love Him" (1:3-4,12).

"Blessed is a man who endures trials, because when he passes the test he will receive the crown of life that He has promised to those who love Him."
James 1:12

James presented a specific Old Testament example—Job's endurance.The Greek word for "endurance" differs from the word for "patience" used in verses 7-10. In those verses "patience" translates "long-suffering," indicating a self-restraint that does not retaliate. The word used twice in

Notes

verse 11, however, means "to endure under hardship," literally "to remain under."

The term used in verse 11 has the idea of staying the course in difficult circumstances. James chose this word to describe Job instead of the one meaning long-suffering because Job did not show the latter (despite the popular phrase "the patience of Job").

Job instead complained openly and bitterly to God about his suffering and its injustice. Yet despite his heart-felt complaints, Job never stopped trusting God. He determined to endure his situation without losing his faith. He exemplified steadfast endurance in a time of great suffering.

We often see such trust and patience in the suffering of the saints of the Lord in our churches. Generally they are older and have God's wisdom through much Bible study and prayer. When we go to see them in the hospital or at home, they encourage us instead of our encouraging them! This perspective can only come from steadfast endurance.

The words "outcome from the Lord" translates literally as "the end of the Lord." Many scholars see "end" in this context as meaning "conclusion." If so, the reference is to how God treated Job in the end because of his perseverance. God enabled Job to understand more fully the Lord's majesty and sovereignty, restored his wealth, and gave him more children.

Others, however, believe "end" means "purpose or design." If so, God's purpose in allowing Job to suffer was to help him mature (1:4). Indeed, Job enjoyed his most intimate fellowship with God in the midst of his trials

On the basis of God's dealing with Job, James described the Lord as "very compassionate and merciful." The word for "compassionate" literally means "large-hearted." "Mercy" is similar in meaning. James used these terms to emphasize God's nature. Out of His tender mercies God provides believers the strength to endure and He rewards their endurance. At the end of it all we will affirm gloriously that the price we paid for remaining faithful was absolutely worthwhile.

"Because of the LORD's great love we are not consumed, for his compassions never fail. They are new every morning; great is your faithfulness."
Lamentations 3:22-23, NIV

Content Points

1. The suffering and patience of Old Testament prophets should be an example and encouragement to us.
2. Perseverance ultimately brings blessing.
3. Despite Job's complaining, Job endured his trials without losing his faith. He is another example to us.
4. Through the maturing process and the blessings received, we will come through the trials with the realization that they were worthwhile.

Discussion Questions

1. Can you remember a difficult time in your life that you were later able to look upon with "20/20 hindsight" and realize how God was working in and through your life?
2. Is there someone in the Bible, in history, or in your life who has been an inspiration and encouragement to you in trying times? What is it about that person that has influenced you?
3. Read 2 Corinthians 1:3-5. How can God use our trials to bless others?

Application Ideas

1. The people, stories, and wisdom of the Bible can only help and encourage you if Scripture is in your head and in your heart. Spend regular time in God's Word in good times so you'll be ready for the hard times.
2. Make 3 listsof times God delivered
   - someone in the Bible
   - someone in history

   someone you know personally
3. When has God strengthened and delivered you?
4. Read 2 Timothy 4:17-18 in the margin. Notice how God's deliverance in the past gave Paul confidence that God would deliver him in the future. Now look back over the lists you made. Use these events to remind and encourage you that God will see you through trials just as He has done for others in the past.
5. Reread 2 Corinthians 1:3 in the margin. Have you experienced God as "the Father of mercies and the God of all comfort"? Are you ready to claim that as a promise, looking to Him and resting in Him when trials come?

"Blessed be the God and Father of our Lord Jesus Christ, the Father of mercies and the God of all comfort. He comforts us in all our affliction, so that we may be able to comfort those who are in any kind of affliction, through the comfort we ourselves receive from God. For as the sufferings of Christ overflow to us, so our comfort overflows through Christ."
2 Corinthians 1:3-5

"But the Lord stood with me and strengthened me, so that the proclamation might be fully made through me, and all the Gentiles might hear. So I was rescued from the lion's mouth. The Lord will rescue me from every evil work and will bring me safely into His heavenly kingdom."
2 Timothy 4:17-18

[12]Now above all, my brothers, do not swear, either by heaven or by earth or with any other oath. Your "yes" must be "yes," and your "no" must be "no," so that you won't fall under judgment.

IV. Endure Patiently As You Speak (v. 12)

"Now above all" stresses the seriousness and importance of what follows because this matter demands the highest priority. It involves the blasphemous use of the name of the Most High God.

The words "do not swear" do not refer to profanity or crude language, though other Scriptures forbid that. Verse 12 refers to swearing an oath. We are to behave and speak in such a way that our simple yes and no will be accepted by everyone without requiring or expecting any oaths.

"But I tell you, don't take an oath at all: either by heaven, because it is God's throne; or by the earth, because it is His footstool; or by Jerusalem, because it is the city of the great King. Neither should you swear by your head, because you cannot make a single hair white or black. But let your word 'yes' be 'yes,' and your 'no' be 'no.' Anything more than this is from the evil one."
Matthew 5:34-37

Notes

"*Since you put away lying, speak the truth, each one to his neighbor, because we are members of one another.*" Ephesians 4:25

We would all like to have patience if we could find it on sale, but we don't like to pay full price for it.

In James's day, swearing an oath in God's name was the strongest guarantee anyone could make. Deceitful and dishonest people often would swear instead by earth or by heaven. We believers should do better than that; we are always to speak truth.

James was not forbidding legal oaths, such as in a courtroom setting. After all, Jesus seems to have agreed to be put on oath in Caiaphas's courtroom (Matt. 26:63-64), and Paul deemed it fitting in his writings to make oaths (Rom. 1:9; 2 Cor. 1:23; Gal. 1:20; Phil. 1:8). The practice clearly was permitted in the Old Testament (Deut. 6:13; Isa. 65:16). However, Jesus condemned the scheming methods of the Pharisees to make some oaths binding and some not (see Matt. 23:16-22).

Sometimes our impatience can lead us to say things that aren't true in an effort to ease the pressure we feel. A young mother entered a doctor's office with a sick child and noticed more than a dozen patients in the waiting room. "The doctor will be with you shortly," said the receptionist.

"Are all these people ahead of me?" she asked.

"Well, yes," the receptionist admitted. "The doctor was called to the hospital for an emergency."

"Then why did you tell me he'd be right with me?" the mother asked.

The receptionist sheepishly replied, "I guess it's easier to say that than to tell the truth and make patients mad at me."

We've all known the temptation to be less than truthful when we are in a difficult spot. James's admonition is always to speak the truth, even if it means we must endure more difficulties.

To fail to do so brings us "under judgment" (Jas. 5:12). Remember, Jesus said, "On the day of judgment people will have to account for every careless word they speak. For by your words you will be acquitted, and by your words you will be condemned" (Matt. 12:36-37).

Endurance and patience are two tough words. Endurance conjures up pictures of sweaty athletes grimacing in pain as they push toward the finish line. We would all like to have patience if we could find it on sale, but we don't like to pay full price for it.

We know patience can be acquired only during seasons of discomfort and even agony, and we often go out of our way to avoid such experiences. James addressed these two characteristics of a mature faith in 5:7-12 to encourage believers in distress not to give up.

Review the whole of chapter 5. Take this message from God to heart. Recommit yourself to living for Christ, regardless of the cost. Trust that in His time and way, He will set all things right.

Content Points

1. "Do not swear" refers to making an oath as a witness to what you are saying.
2. As Christians, our lives should be the witness to the truth of what we say. We shouldn't need to make an oath to distinguish what really is the truth.
3. We condemn ourselves when we make an oath because we confess that our words are not always truthful.

Discussion Questions

1. How does making an oath reflect on our character?
2. Why did James say that anything beyond a "yes" or "no" will bring judgment?

Application Ideas

1. Does your life vouch for the truth of your words? When you speak, are people confident that they can believe you?
2. Read Matthew 12:37. Do your words acquit or condemn you? How should the teaching of Jesus and James affect your speech?

"For by your words you will be acquitted, and by your words you will be condemned." Matthew 12:37

SUMMARY

1. James 5:1-6 and 5:7-12 address two different groups of people: The wealthy who abuse the poor receive harsh words in 5:1-6 and those who are abused receive comforting words in 5:7-12.

2. Wealth can be abused in at least four ways:
   - accumulation (how much we have)
   - appropriation (how we got it)
   - allocation (how we spend it)
   - application (how much money buys influence)

3. We should gain strength to endure trying times through the knowledge that Jesus is coming again and that God is in control in the meantime.

4. Using the example of the Old Testament saints, James tells us that we will be blessed when we endure times of trial. Such endurance brings spiritual maturity and ultimately, the crown of life (see 1:3-4,12).

5. Failure to consistently speak the truth will bring us under God's judgment (Matt. 12:36-37).

Notes

[5]You have lived luxuriously on the land and have indulged yourselves. You have fattened your hearts for the day of slaughter.

Going Deeper— Financial Responsibility

Scripture teaches that we are responsible for making a living, that is, for providing the material needs necessary for life. For most of us, that means we need to earn money by working. Diligent work and disciplined spending often result in a measure of affluence, meaning we have more than enough to provide life's necessities. In each culture or society "affluence" is a relative term, and our material wants generally tend to outstrip our earnings. Each of us, therefore, must determine prayerfully an acceptable "standard of living." Here are a few basic biblical teachings that can help us do so responsibly:

1. *We are responsible to God for doing "honest work" (Eph. 4:28).*
2. *We are responsible to God for giving a tithe or one-tenth of our earnings to the Lord through His church (Lev. 27:30).*
3. *We are responsible to God for providing for our families and, as needed, for our extended family (1 Tim. 5:8).*
4. *We are responsible to God for sharing generously our money with people in need (Acts 20:35).*

[7]Therefore, brothers, be patient until the Lord's coming. See how the farmer waits for the precious fruit of the earth and is patient with it until it receives the early and the late rains. [8]You also must be patient. Strengthen your hearts, because the Lord's coming is near.

Going Deeper: New Testament Terms for Christ's Second Coming

The second coming of Christ (a phrase not found in the Bible) is expressed in the New Testament in the following special terms:

1. Parousia, *a fairly common Greek word, means "presence" (Phil 2:12). More especially it may mean presence after absence. Archaeological discoveries explain why the word received such general Christian use to describe Christ's second coming. The term was used for the arrival of a ruler at* a particular place. Consequently, Greek-speaking Christians naturally adopted a word that already contained regal and even Divine concepts. It refers to the coming of Christ in 1 Corinthians 15:23; 1 Thessalonians 2:19; 3:13; 4:15; 5:23; 2 Thessalonians 2:1,8; James 5:7-8; 2 Peter 1:16; 3:4,12; and 1 John 2:28.

2. Epiphany *(epiphaneia), means "manifestation." This word is used of Christ's incarnation in 2 Timothy 1:10, but it speaks of the Second Coming in 2 Thessalonians 2:8; 1 Timothy 6:14; 2 Timothy 4:1,8; and Titus 2:13. The word was used like parousia to denote the ceremonial arrival of rulers.*

3. Apocalypse *(apokalupsis), meaning "revelation," denotes the Second Coming in 1 Corinthians 1:7; 2 Thessalonians 1:7; and 1 Peter 1:7,13; 4:13.*

4. Day of the Lord, more or less modified, refers to Christ's return in 1 Corinthians 1:8; 5:5; 2 Corinthians 1:14; Philippians 1:6,10; 2:16; 1 Thessalonians 5:2; and 2 Thessalonians 2:2.

1. Available from the Internet: *www.generousgiving.org*
2. Counsel on Foundations [online], 2007 [cited 13 March 2007]. Available from the Internet: *http://www.cof.org/learn/content.cfm?ItemNumber=862&navItemNumber=2264*
3. Charles Edward White, "What Wesley Preached and Practiced About Money," [online] [cited 13 March 2007]. Available from the Internet: *http://www.urbana.org/_articles.cfm?RecordId=435*

JAMES 5:13-20 (HCSB)

*[13]Is anyone among you suffering? He should pray. Is anyone
cheerful? He should sing praises. [14]Is anyone among you sick?
He should call for the elders of the church, and they should
pray over him after anointing him with olive oil in the name of
the Lord. [15]The prayer of faith will save the sick person, and the
Lord will raise him up; and if he has committed sins, he will be
forgiven. [16]Therefore, confess your sins to one another and pray
for one another, so that you may be healed. The intense prayer of
the righteous is very powerful. [17]Elijah was a man with a nature
like ours; yet he prayed earnestly that it would not rain, and for
three years and six months it did not rain on the land. [18]Then he
prayed again, and the sky gave rain and the land produced its
fruit.*

*[19]My brothers, if any among you strays from the truth, and
someone turns him back, [20]he should know that whoever turns a
sinner from the error of his way will save his life from death and
cover a multitude of sins.*

Lesson Eight

PRAY CONFIDENTLY (JAMES 5:13-20)

I. Pray Confidently About Suffering (5:13-15)

II. Pray Confidently About Sin and Forgiveness (5:16)

III. Pray Confidently About Other Situations (5:16-18)

IV. Pray Confidently About Those Who Stray (5:19-20)

LEARNING GOALS

As a result of studying this session, learners will:

- *Identify occasions that call for prayer*
- *Grasp the responsibilities and importance of praying for the sick*
- *Explain the possible relationship between illness and sin and the scope of confession*
- *Affirm God's power to answer the prayers of ordinary people*
- *Accept the responsibility of prayerfully participating in the ministry of restoration*

Notes

You may have heard about the man who was flying his small plane. He called the control tower and said, "Pilot to tower, I'm 60 miles from the airport, 600 feet above the ground, and I'm out of fuel. I am descending rapidly. Please advise, Over." Immediately came this reply: "Tower to pilot, repeat after me: 'Our Father who art in heaven.'"

Where did we ever get the idea that prayer is only to be used as a last resort? Have we been influenced by the old stock movie scene in which the doctor says to the family in the waiting room, "I'm sorry; I've done everything I can. All we can do now is pray"? Or do we trust more in our own efforts until we become extremely desperate?

At least 75 verses in the New Testament have something to say about prayer. Even the most casual reading of Scripture reveals that prayer was a major part of the life and ministry of Jesus and became the power source for those in the early church. Prayer is a first resource, not a last resort.

What do you believe about prayer? Perhaps the most accurate answer to that question is found in your practice of prayer. Praying is mentioned seven times in James 5:13-20. Being able to talk to God is the greatest privilege of the Christian life. He is the source of power for our Christian living and service. Not praying, therefore, is frequently behind our greatest failures as believers. We talk a lot about prayer, and we study about prayer; yet many of us are sadly deficient in our prayer life. May this lesson on prayer stimulate us to put a renewed priority on prayer.

[13]Is anyone among you suffering? He should pray. Is anyone cheerful? He should sing praises. [14]Is anyone among you sick? He should call for the elders of the church, and they should pray over him after anointing him with olive oil in the name of the Lord. [15]The prayer of faith will save the sick person, and the Lord will raise him up; and if he has committed sins, he will be forgiven.

I. Pray Confidently About Suffering (v. 13-15)

With three rhetorical questions in verses 13-14 James expressed concern for seriously troubled believers. All of us at times experience suffering. The Greek word for "suffering" (v. 13) is composed of two words, "evil" and "to suffer." It refers to any kind of difficulty or painful experience—sickness, bereavement, disappointment, persecution, and loss of health or property. This is the term James used in verse 10 to describe the kind of trouble the Old Testament prophets experienced as a consequence of obeying the Lord.

Helpless poor people in the early church lived in a world filled with distress and worry. James could not relieve their material difficulties, but he reminded them of the resource of prayer. The force of the verb "should pray" is "should keep on praying." Prayer represents a positive, active response to trials instead of fighting or seeking revenge.

Prayer may not result in the removal of troubles. When we ask God to remove the cause of our difficulties, we are to follow Jesus' model of declaring "not My will, but Yours, be done" (Luke 22:42). We can pray for strength to endure hardships, asking God to transform our attitudes toward the situation or the people involved. Habitual prayer, which James was advising, can transform us in our troubles even if it does not end our troubles.

"Let us continually offer up to God a sacrifice of praise, that is, the fruit of our lips that confess His name." Hebrews 13:15

The Christian life, while difficult, is not dismal. James anticipated that believers often would be "cheerful" (v. 13). "Cheerful" describes a state of mind opposite that of anxiety and distress caused by suffering of some kind. So what should we do when we are happy? Some celebrate joyful occasions by drinking. A sports bar owner declared business was a lot better after a local sporting event when the home team won rather than lost.

"Speak to one another with psalms, hymns and spiritual songs. Sing and make music in your heart to the Lord, always giving thanks to God the Father for everything, in the name of our Lord Jesus Christ." Ephesians 5:19-20, NIV

James had another activity in mind. When we are cheerful, we are "to sing praises," either with or without an instrument. The reference is to any songs of praise, including any we might make up on our own. Praise is a form of prayer, and these praises acknowledge God as the source of every "perfect gift" (1:17). Praise expresses grateful joy that also helps us keep close to God.

James specified a particular cause of suffering in his teaching about prayer—sickness. Minor and major illnesses typically are simply a fact of life for all of us, believers and unbelievers alike. The word translated "sick" in verse 14 literally means "without strength." It describes one who is totally wasted, fatigued, bedridden, and thus unable to work. The sick person is instructed to "call for the elders of the church" to come and pray for him.

Verse 14 assumes two things. **First**, believers belong to a local church. Some claim not to believe in organized religion. The church is an organism, not an organization. It is an expression of the body of Christ, and each of us believers are members of it. When we are sick or have some other need, we have pastors, deacons, teachers, and other brothers and sisters on whom we can call for help.

Second, verse 14 also assumes the sick person is responsible for initiating contact with the church. A woman whose pastor did not visit her when she was severely ill told a deacon, "The pastor doesn't care about little folk like me." The friend responded with a twinkle in his eye, "Maude, if he don't know, he can't go."

Notes

The earlier English translation of "elders" used "presbyter," a transliteration of the Greek word (changing Greek alphabet letters to English letters). The word literally refers to older people, implying people who are more mature and experienced. "Elders" in verse 14 refers to church leaders. Perhaps from among these respected mature believers the church chose their pastors and deacons as well.

Three instructions are given to the church leaders. **First,** they are to anoint him with olive oil. Bible scholars have suggested two main interpretations on anointing the sick with oil. Some see it as a reference to medicine. The people of ancient times used olive oil as medicine (see the parable of the good Samaritan, Luke 10:34). Others view the anointing with oil as symbolic of God's faithful concern to help His children in time of need. Although a different Greek verb typically describes symbolical or sacred anointing, both interpretations seem valid.

The **second** instruction is to do the anointing "in the name of the Lord." God is the healer, not any person. The "name" represents the character of the Lord. All healing is based on God's character—His love, righteousness, wisdom, grace, and mercy. **Third,** "pray over Him." James 5:15 states the results of praying for the sick and provides grounds for praying with great confidence—"The prayer of faith will save the sick person, and the Lord will raise him up; and if he has committed sins, he will be forgiven." In this context the word "save" indicates healing rather than salvation—"The Lord will raise him up" from his sickbed. The use of "if" acknowledges, however, that sickness may be a result of an individual's sins. (See Mark 2:1-12).

A number of churches carry out James's instructions literally. During an extended illness, seriously ill members have asked ministers and godly leaders to come, anoint them with olive oil, and pray for them. Those participating always testify of a powerful time of worship. God is, of course, responsible for any healing that occurs; but He works through prayers of faithful people. While He certainly uses medicines as a means of His healing, many healings defy natural explanations.

We all know of some sick folk who fervently were prayed for but who did not experience healing. This verse raises the question, Why isn't everybody healed? The short and honest answer is that we do not know. God has the power to heal, but apparently God's purpose in many cases is not to heal.

A clear example of this is the experience Paul described in 2 Corinthians 12:7-10. Paul prayed three times for God to remove what seems to have been a chronic health problem. God responded in effect that He would instead enable Paul to serve Him effectively with his problem—"My grace is sufficient for you, for power is perfected in weakness."

How did Paul receive this denial of healing? "Therefore, I will most gladly boast all the more about my weaknesses, so that Christ's power may reside in me. So because of Christ, I am pleased in weaknesses, in insults, in catastrophes, in persecutions, and in pressures. For when I am weak, then I am strong" (2 Cor. 12:9-10). Paul's response provides a model for us. God does not always reveal His reasons, but He always meets our needs in one way or another. Thus we can rely on His love and wisdom whether we ever understand the precise purpose of our suffering.

Content Points

1. The word translated "suffering" (HCSB) or "trouble" (NIV) refers to any kind of difficulty or painful experience—sickness, bereavement, disappointment, persecution, and loss of health or property.
2. A healthy prayer life can transform us in our troubles even if it does not end our troubles.
3. James instructed the sick to ask (showing faith) their church leaders to pray for them "in the name of the Lord" (in His authority) for healing and forgiveness.
4. God has all power to heal, but we must acknowledge that all healing is according to His will and purposes.

Discussion Questions

1. Other than pray, what are we likely to do when we encounter difficulty?
2. What does "singing praises" reveal about our relationship with God?
3. Why do we not ask for healing prayer as James instructed?
4. What did Paul mean when he said, "When I am weak, then I am strong"?

Application Ideas

1. Prayer should be a way of life in all circumstances, not just when we are suffering or as a last resort.
2. When you pray, do you really believe that God will answer?
3. Are you guilty of exhausting every alternative before "resorting" to prayer?
4. The next time you feel weak, focus on God's strength instead of your weakness. Read Psalm 42:5-11.

"I pleaded with the Lord three times to take it away from me. But He said to me, 'My grace is sufficient for you, for power is perfected in weakness.' Therefore, I will most gladly boast all the more about my weaknesses, so that Christ's power may reside in me. So because of Christ, I am pleased in weaknesses, in insults, in catastrophes, in persecutions, and in pressures. For when I am weak, then I am strong."
2 Corinthians 12:8-10

Notes

"When I kept silent, my bones became brittle from my groaning all day long. Then I acknowledged my sin to You and did not conceal my iniquity. I said, 'I will confess my transgressions to the LORD,' and You took away the guilt of my sin." Psalm 32:3,5

"If we confess our sins, He is faithful and righteous to forgive us our sins and to cleanse us from all unrighteousness." 1 John 1:9

16Therefore, confess your sins to one another and pray for one another, so that you may be healed. The intense prayer of the righteous is very powerful.

II. *Pray Confidently About Sin and Forgiveness* (v. 16)

In Jesus' day people tended to assume that a person's sickness was a result of that person's sin. Jesus dismissed that idea in John 9:3 by explaining a man's blindness was not caused by his sins or the sins of anyone else. We live in a world suffering from the accumulated results of sin. Unfortunately, some people tend to forget John 9:3 and draw wrong conclusions.

On the other hand, we certainly can act in ways that bring sickness on ourselves. Violating God-given principles of health over time can lead to serious ailments. He designed us physically so that we need to eat healthy foods, get adequate sleep, and exercise properly to maintain health. Medical researchers have also demonstrated the long-term physical and mental damage that result from ignoring spiritual principles such as forgiveness, kindness, and generosity. Harboring resentment, hatred, grudges, and envy are detrimental to our health.

Regardless of the cause of one's illness, a meeting of concerned believers around a sick bed can provide an effective opportunity for confession, repentance, and forgiveness. The word translated "confess" means "to say the same thing." For instance, God's Word teaches that failing to forgive others is a sin. To confess an unforgiving spirit means we say what God says; that is, we admit our refusal to forgive is a sin.

We stop trying to justify the sin to ourselves and to others. We throw away our list of reasons never to forgive that person. Acknowledging our sins to fellow believers allows them to pray more specifically for us, and it frees us to turn to God in repentance and to receive His forgiveness.

James said to confess sins; however, do not broadcast them. We should confess all our sins according to a principle some call the circle of confession. It says, "Only confess as widely as the sin involves other people." If we commit a sin that's only between the Lord and ourselves, then we ought to confess it only to the Lord. If it is a sin that impacted another individual, then we need to confess it to that person, seeking the person's forgiveness, as well as God's forgiveness. If it is a public sin, then we need to confess it to God and apologize to the whole church.

Confession also is appropriate when we need the support of other Christians to overcome particular temptations with which we struggle. Let us confess our sins but always use wisdom and discretion about what and to whom we confess.

Content Points

1. Jesus taught sickness did not directly result from sin.
2. Sin, as well as neglect, can result in sickness.
3. Spiritual sickness—such as anger, bitterness, and unforgiveness—can literally make us sick.
4. Confession is agreeing with God about our sin, acknowledging it, and seeking His forgiveness.
5. In order to help us overcome the temptation to sin again we should confess our sins to others who are impacted by our sins .

Discussion Questions

1. How do spiritual sins literally make us sick?
2. Why are we reluctant to confess our sins to others?
3. How can confessing our sins to another person (not just God) help us overcome that sin?

Application Ideas

1. Are you harboring sinful attitudes that affect you spiritually? Physically? If so, do you ever confess your sins to another person? If not, why?
2. Read Mark 7:21-22; Romans 1:29-30,32; Galatians 5:19-21; Colossians 3:5,8-9. Use these lists as prompts for actions or attitudes you need to confess. Note the warnings in Romans 1:32 and Galatians 5:21.
3. Consider asking a close Christian friend to be your accountability partner. Define up front the freedom and limits you are giving each other to ask tough questions and hold each other accountable in your walk.

[16]Therefore, confess your sins to one another and pray for one another, so that you may be healed. The intense prayer of the righteous is very powerful. [17]Elijah was a man with a nature like ours; yet he prayed earnestly that it would not rain, and for three years and six months it did not rain on the land. [18]Then he prayed again, and the sky gave rain and the land produced its fruit.

III. *Pray Confidently About Other Situations* (vv. 16-18)

The latter part of verse 16 widens the responsibility of intercessory prayer to include believers in general—"The intense prayer of the righteous is very powerful." In addition to prayers for the sick and the straying (vv. 19-20), all of us need to give and receive prayer support of our fellow believers. The word translated "prayer" carries the idea of "petition or supplication." The exhortation to pray is strengthened by affirming the effective power of prayer. Those who pray effectively are among "the righteous."

A Confession & Repentance Checklist for Mind & Mouth

greed
stinginess
envy
jealousy
selfish ambition
pride
deception
lying
filthy language
obscenity
foolish talk
crude joking
blasphemy
lust
lewdness
foolishness
malice
gossip
slander
hatred
anger
wrath
bitterness
discord
dissension
evil desires

(from Mark 7:21-22; Romans 1:29-30,32; Galatians 5:19-21; Colossians 3:5,8-9)

Notes

"Now this is the confidence we have before Him: whenever we ask anything according to His will, He hears us. And if we know that He hears whatever we ask, we know that we have what we have asked Him for." 1 John 5:14-15

"Then Elijah became afraid and immediately ran for his life. When he came to Beer-sheba ... He sat down under a broom tree and prayed that he might die. He said, 'I have had enough! LORD, *take my life.'"* 1 Kings 19:3-4

"Devote yourselves to prayer; stay alert in it with thanksgiving." Colossians 4:2

Righteous people depend on God and seek to pray according to God's will with urgency, earnestness, and energy.

However, "is very powerful" can be translated in various ways—"availeth much" (KJV); "has great power in its effects" (RSV); "is powerful and effective" (NIV). Though translations differ, the promise is clear. When those who are righteous petition God on behalf of another, marvelous blessings follow. God uses such praying to accomplish His purposes.

Some of us believers think we have to be spiritual giants to pray and receive God-sized answers. We may say to ourselves, "I could never pray and see somebody healed;" or "I could never pray and see a financial turn-around." James was aware of the challenge to faith his words on prayer posed, so he used Elijah as an illustration in verses 17-18.

We might question whether Elijah is an appropriate illustration to encourage "ordinary" believers to trust God to answer prayers. Elijah was a ninth century B.C. prophet of the Northern Kingdom and the earliest of Israel's great prophets. Later generations thought of Elijah as being semi-divine because of the miracles God performed through him. James dispelled the notion that Elijah was a spiritual Superman by affirming, "Elijah was a man with a nature like ours."

Literally the word translated "with a nature like" means "suffering the same frailties as." He was subject to fatigue, discouragement, and depression as we all are. After the contest with the prophets of Baal on Mount Carmel, a glorious victory of faith, Ahab and Jezebel were still king and queen. Jezebel sentenced him to death. Elijah fled into the desert, and in his depression he prayed for God to take his life (1 Kings 19). Elijah demonstrated fear, resentment, guilt, anger, loneliness, and worry. Since God answered Elijah's prayers despite his human frailties, He also will answer ours.

We might mistakenly conclude Elijah was a spiritual wimp. Let us review the background to James's illustration. Elijah burst on the biblical scene after Ahab had assumed the throne of Israel and became the nation's most wicked king. Ahab allowed Queen Jezebel to promote Baal worship throughout the land. James indicated that Elijah's response was to pray for God to punish His people's idolatry with drought. Trusting God to answer his prayer, Elijah boldly prophesied to Ahab in the name of the Lord that neither dew nor rain would fall in the land until he asked God to break the drought (17:1). God answered Elijah's prayer.

In the third year after the drought began, God told Elijah to return to Ahab. God also informed Elijah that He was about to send rain on the land again. Elijah returned to Ahab and arranged a contest between himself and the prophets of Baal to prove whose God was real. After those prophets were defeated, Elijah told Ahab the rains were coming (18:41). Sure that the rain was just ahead, Elijah "went up to the summit of Carmel; he bowed down to the ground and put his face between his knees" (v. 42). He prayed on the basis of God's promise to send rain, so He was praying according to God's will. The drought ended.

Look at the example of Elijah. First Kings 18 tells of his praying for rain. He prayed seven times. He was persistent. He would not give up. In God's timing, the rains came in a deluge. God works through the prayers of ordinary people to do extraordinary things. Let us pray in faith like Elijah.

Thoughtful readers of Scripture have asked the reason James said the time of drought was "three years and six months" (Jas. 5:17) when 1 Kings 18:1 said the drought ended "in the third year." The phrase in 1 Kings probably refers to the end of the third year after the rain ceased to fall. Rains ordinarily fell there in two seasons—October and April (the "early" and "latter" rains). A six month interval thus separated the two seasons of rain. Adding those six months to the full three years without rain gives "three years and six months." Jesus also said the drought and its resulting famine lasted "three years and six months" (Luke 4:25.)

The same Spirit of God who worked through Elijah indwells every believer. The lesson of Elijah's life is this: we do not have to be perfect to pray and receive answers to our prayers. Because we never know perfectly God's purposes, we may or may not see immediate answers to our prayers.

"Pray at all times and on every occasion in the power of the Holy Spirit. Stay alert and be persistent in your prayers for all Christians everywhere."
Ephesians 6:18, NLT

Content Points

1. Righteous people depend on God and seek to live according to His demands.
2. God uses the prayers of His earnest followers to accomplish great things.
3. Yes, Elijah was a great prophet, but he was a man with weaknesses and failings as well. God can use you, just like He used Elijah, to accomplish His purposes.

Discussion Questions

1. Why do we think that miraculous prayer is only for the "super saints" of the Bible?
2. Who qualifies as a "righteous man" (or woman)?
3. What might God do through us if we were obedient to pray persistently for His will to be done?

Application Ideas

1. Are you righteous? Many do not want to claim that they qualify. What did Jesus do that qualifies us?
2. Do you see answers to your prayers that are clearly "God things"?
3. Rate your prayer life based on prayer for others instead of yourself/your family, What would you circle:
   infrequent sometimes usually always

Notes

"Watch out, brothers, so that there won't be in any of you an evil, unbelieving heart that departs from the living God. But encourage each other daily, while it is still called today, so that none of you is hardened by sin's deception." Hebrews 3:12-13

"Brothers, if someone is caught in any wrongdoing, you who are spiritual should restore such a person with a gentle spirit, watching out for yourselves so you won't be tempted also." Galatians 6:1

"[God] wants everyone to be saved and to come to the knowledge of the truth." 1 Timothy 2:4

[19]My brothers, if any among you strays from the truth, and someone turns him back, [20]he should know that whoever turns a sinner from the error of his way will save his life from death and cover a multitude of sins.

IV. *Pray Confidently About Those Who Stray* (vv. 19-20)

As James addressed various issues throughout his letter, his overall purpose was to encourage believers to hold to the faith and to live by it. In verses 19-20 he encourages us to restore those who stray from the Lord. The words "if any among you" (v. 19) make plain the reference is to straying believers. These verses stress that prodigals matter to God, so they also should matter to us. "Someone" in verse 20 shows that reclaiming a believer who has fallen into sin is the duty of all Christians, not just church leaders.

Why are so many of us reluctant to make the effort? Our cultural influence tells us, "Mind your own business—who do you think you are to correct someone else?" Add to that the general lack of accountability we have to one another—along with the false belief that religious faith is a private matter—and we can understand why such reluctance exists.

However, we must take to heart the biblical mandate to restore one another. Ezekiel 34:16 says, "I will seek the lost, bring back the strays, bandage the injured, and strengthen the weak." Jesus said in Luke 17:3, "Be on your guard. If your brother sins, rebuke him; and if he repents, forgive him." Paul told Timothy to "proclaim the message; persist in it whether convenient or not; rebuke, correct, and encourage with great patience and teaching" (2 Tim. 4:2). Our motives must be love , concern, and obedience, not a desire to humiliate. We must never consider ourselves above rebuke or our efforts to restore the wandering brother or sister will be futile.

Take a closer look at James 5:19-20. "My brothers" is one of James's tender expressions. He was concerned about the welfare of all churches and of all their members. The thought that he and they all were brothers and sisters in Christ seems to have been special to him. In the Old Testament, "brother," like "neighbor," was used only of a fellow Israelite. The foundation for their sense of kinship was a common ancestry.

Most of the New Testament writers used "brother" and "sister" to refer to the close, spiritual kinship believers have in Christ, whether Jews or Gentiles. That it was a treasured kinship is shown by James's use of the singular—"any among you [who] strays from the truth."

James approached this subject delicately. The wording indicates a supposed case, not a particular one. The verb for "strays," when used in its passive form, suggests the straying ones may have been deceived or misled into their straying. The term presents the picture of a person who has lost his or her way and goes about aimlessly. James suggested these believers were not necessarily gone for good and could be turned "back" into safe spiritual territory—back to "the truth."

"Truth" can refer to what we believe (doctrine), how we act (morals), or both. Throughout the letter James had insisted believers live by the truth, not merely profess it. Genuine faith issues forth in works. Straying from the truth could be intellectual, moral, or doctrinal. When believers do not follow closely enough the One who is Himself the truth, they are vulnerable to teachings that sound good but are deceitfully false (John 14:6).

"If we claim to have fellowship with him yet walk in the darkness, we lie and do not live by the truth." 1 John 1:6, NIV

Faithful brothers and sisters have some options in dealing with the problem of straying members. For instance, we could kick them out, abandon and ignore them, or reach out to them in an effort to turn them back. James gave his readers strong encouragement to choose this last option.

James wanted all of us to "know" the immense importance of making efforts to bring the straying back into the fold. Verse 20 magnifies the reality that turning aside from the Christian way of life is no light matter. Reclaiming straying Christians turns a sinner from the error of his way, saves his life from death, and covers a multitude of sins.

Bible scholars have differing opinions of the meaning of "death" in verse 20. Some conclude James was referring to unbelievers and speaking of their salvation from eternal spiritual death. Yet the context indicates that James was addressing Christians. Perhaps James was implying that those who refused to turn back to God were not actually believers. Of course, only God knows who truly has trusted in Christ and who has made an empty claim of faith. "Whoever turns a sinner from the error of his way" is the brother or sister who understands that the only life worth living is the life lived in Christ.

"If your brother sins against you, go and rebuke him in private. If he listens to you, you have won your brother. But if he won't listen, take one or two more with you, so that by the testimony of two or three witnesses every fact may be established. If he pays no attention to them, tell the church." Matthew 18:15-17

The moment we see professed believers being misled is the moment we are to begin the effort to turn them from the error of their way. This ongoing responsibility involves unfailing intercessory prayer and unwavering love expressed in gentle, caring ways. If successful, we can "save [a] life from death." We can "save"? Yes, but only in a limited sense.

Only God saves eternally, but sometimes He will use Christians to turn back other Christians who have wandered. The reclaiming of one who strays covers "a multitude of sins." This vivid image of God's forgiveness suggests sins are hidden from God's sight. "Multitude" points to the great extent of this forgiveness. God's grace is greater than any or all of our sins. The psalmist declared the person "blessed" whose sins are covered (Ps. 32:1). Again, only God can save from death.

"How happy is the one whose transgression is forgiven, whose sin is covered! How happy is the man the LORD does not charge with sin, and in whose spirit is no deceit!" Psalm 32:1-2

In many places today, as in James's day, some believers' lives and livelihood are in peril if they remain true to their Christian commitment. Most of us reading this lesson do not face

Notes

"Pray at all times." Ephesians 6:18

"Pray constantly." 1 Thessalonians 5:17

that extreme level of pressure. Instead, the straying believers among us are often led astray by the lure of immoral pleasure, the anger of wounded pride, the appeal of worldly philosophy, and the desire to be accepted in more so-called sophisticated circles.

Check to see who on your church membership role is "inactive" and who still live in your community. Pray for them and ask God to work in their hearts and to guide you in ways He may want to use you in a ministry of reclamation.

Content Points

1. Christians have a biblical mandate to reach out to fellow Christians who have strayed into sin.
2. The goal in church discipline is always restoration, not humiliation.
3. Turning a straying Christian back to the faith is a matter of life and death.

Discussion Questions

1. Why are we so reluctant to confront other believers about their sin?
2. Why is seeking to bring back straying Christians so important?

Application Ideas

1. Have you ever confronted a fellow Christian over his or her sin? Is there someone with whom you need to talk about something inappropriate in his or her life?
3. How might you refute the implication that you are judging this individual? (See Lesson Six.)

SUMMARY

1. We should pray for many things such as victory in temptation, forgiveness, suffering, and sickness.

2. Prayers of righteous believers are powerful. Prayers of faith bring healing to the sick and forgiveness of sin.

3. Although Jesus told us that sickness is not a direct result of sin (John 9:3), physical and emotional neglect or abuse of our bodies can result in sickness.

4. Elijah was an "ordinary man" just like you and me, and God used his prayers to accomplish amazing things.

5. Reclaiming believers who have fallen into sin is the duty of all Christians, not just church leaders.

[14]Is anyone among you sick? He should call for the elders of the church, and they should pray over him after anointing him with olive oil in the name of the Lord.

Going Deeper—Elders (5:14)

In ancient times, people naturally looked to those who were older and thus more experienced as leaders. Later, the term "elder" came to refer not only to age but also to dignity and authority. In the New Testament this title was one of those given to the office of pastor. From the Greek word translated "elder" we derive the English word "presbyter," a title calling attention to the spiritual maturity and experience those who hold this office should exemplify. These church leaders are commanded to act as "shepherds" over God's flock, a designation pointing to the sacrificial care and spiritual feeding a pastor should provide to believers (see Acts 20:28).

Another title is "overseer" ("bishop"). This designation focuses on the pastor's responsibility to watch over the flock. Although New Testament writers appear to have used "elder" and "overseer" synonymously, perhaps "elder" refers more to who the person is and "overseer" to what the person does.

In Titus 1:5-9 Paul mentioned both "elder" and "overseer." Peter gave instructions to pastors—"Therefore, as a fellow elder and witness to the sufferings of the Messiah ... I exhort the elders among you: shepherd God's flock among you, not overseeing out of compulsion but freely" (1 Pet. 5:1-2).

Studying the Book of James is profitable only when we are doers of the Word. In these eight lessons we've looked at the effect our faith has on our attitudes during trials and tough situations. We have considered how authentic faith affects our relationships. We've examined the difference between authentic faith and the counterfeit faith that hears God's Word but fails to act on it.

We've been confronted with the importance of keeping a tight rein on our tongues. We've been challenged to examine the motives within us that cause so much of the hurt and pain in our lives. We've been warned about pride, greed, and impatience. We've been encouraged to make prayer the first resort in any situation, not the last resort.

In only 108 verses, we have been challenged in just about every area of life. What new ways have you discovered to integrate your faith into your work, your family, your church, and your social relationships?

In the Christian Growth Study Plan (formerly Church Study Course), this book *LifeWay In-depth Bible Study: James* is a resource for course credit in the subject area Bible Studies of the Christian Growth category of plans. To receive credit, read the book, complete the learning activities, show your work to your pastor, a staff member or church leader, then complete the following information. This page may be duplicated. Send the completed page to:

Christian Growth Study Plan, One LifeWay Plaza
Nashville, TN 37234-0117
FAX: (615)251-5067, E-mail: cgspnet@lifeway.com
For information about the Christian Growth Study Plan, refer to the Christian Growth Study Plan Catalog. It is located online at *www.lifeway.com/cgsp.* If you do not have access to the Internet, contact the Christian Growth Study Plan office (1.800.968.5519) for the specific plan you need for your ministry.

JAMES: HOW TO LIVE BY FAITH IN A SECULAR WORLD

COURSE NUMBER: CG-1198

PARTICIPANT INFORMATION

Social Security Number (USA ONLY-optional) | Personal CGSP Number* | Date of Birth (MONTH, DAY, YEAR)

Name (First, Middle, Last) | Home Phone

Address (Street, Route, or P.O. Box) | City, State, or Province | Zip/Postal Code

Email Address for CGSP use

Please check appropriate box: ❑ Resource purchased by church ❑ Resource purchased by self ❑ Other

CHURCH INFORMATION

Church Name

Address (Street, Route, or P.O. Box) | City, State, or Province | Zip/Postal Code

CHANGE REQUEST ONLY

☐ Former Name

☐ Former Address | City, State, or Province | Zip/Postal Code

☐ Former Church | City, State, or Province | Zip/Postal Code

Signature of Pastor, Conference Leader, or Other Church Leader | Date

*New participants are requested but not required to give SS# and date of birth. Existing participants, please give CGSP# when using SS# for the first time. Thereafter, only one ID# is required. **Mail to:** Christian Growth Study Plan, One LifeWay Plaza, Nashville, TN 37234-0117. Fax: (615)251-5067.

Revised 4-05